DEPARTMENT OF THE TREASURY
TECHNICAL EXPLANATION OF THE
PROTOCOL BETWEEN
THE UNITED STATES OF AMERICA
AND
NEW ZEALAND
SIGNED AT WASHINGTON ON DECEMBER 1, 2008
AMENDING THE CONVENTION AND PROTOCOL BETWEEN
THE UNITED STATES OF AMERICA AND NEW ZEALAND
FOR THE AVOIDANCE OF DOUBLE TAXATION AND
THE PREVENTION OF FISCAL EVASION
WITH RESPECT TO TAXES ON INCOME,
SIGNED AT WELLINGTON ON JULY 23, 1982

DEPARTMENT OF THE TREASURY
TECHNICAL EXPLANATION OF THE
PROTOCOL BETWEEN
THE UNITED STATES OF AMERICA
AND
NEW ZEALAND
SIGNED AT WASHINGTON ON DECEMBER 1, 2008
AMENDING THE CONVENTION AND PROTOCOL BETWEEN
THE UNITED STATES OF AMERICA AND NEW ZEALAND
FOR THE AVOIDANCE OF DOUBLE TAXATION AND
THE PREVENTION OF FISCAL EVASION
WITH RESPECT TO TAXES ON INCOME,
SIGNED AT WELLINGTON ON JULY 23, 1982

This is a technical explanation of the Protocol between the United States and New Zealand signed at Washington on December 1, 2008 (the "Protocol") amending the Convention and Protocol between the United States and New Zealand for the Avoidance of Double Taxation and the Prevention of Fiscal Evasion with Respect to Taxes on Income signed at Wellington on July 23, 1982 (the "existing Convention").

Negotiations took into account the U.S. Treasury Department's current tax treaty policy, and the Treasury Department's Model Income Tax Convention, published on November 15, 2006 (the "U.S. Model"). Negotiations also took into account the Model Tax Convention on Income and on Capital, published by the Organisation for Economic Cooperation and Development (the "OECD Model"), and recent tax treaties concluded by both countries.

The Technical Explanation is an official guide to the Convention. It reflects the policies behind particular Convention provisions, as well as understandings reached during the negotiations with respect to the application and interpretation of the Convention. References to the "existing Convention" are intended to put various provisions of the Protocol into context. The Technical Explanation does not, however, provide a complete comparison between the provisions of the existing Convention and the amendments by the Protocol. The Technical Explanation is not intended to provide a complete guide to the existing Convention as amended by the Protocol. To the extent that a paragraph from the existing Convention has not been amended by the Protocol, the technical explanations to the existing Convention remain the official explanation. References in this Technical Explanation to "he" or "his" should be read to mean "he or she" or "his and her." References to the "Code" are to the Internal Revenue Code of 1986, as amended.

ARTICLE I

Paragraph 1

Article I of the Protocol amends paragraph 3 of Article 1 (General Scope) of the existing Convention.

New paragraph 3 contains the traditional saving clause found in all U.S. tax treaties. The Contracting States reserve their rights, except as provided in paragraph 4, to tax their residents and citizens as provided in their internal laws, notwithstanding any provisions of the Convention to the contrary. For example, if a resident of New Zealand performs professional services in the United States and the income from the services is not attributable to a permanent establishment in the United States, Article 7 (Business Profits) would by its terms prevent the United States from taxing the income. If, however, the resident of New Zealand is also a citizen of the United States, the saving clause permits the United States to include the remuneration in the worldwide income of the citizen and subject it to tax under the normal Code rules (*i.e.*, without regard to Code section 894(a)). However, subparagraph 4(a) of Article 1 preserves the benefits of special foreign tax credit rules applicable to the U.S. taxation of certain U.S. income of its citizens resident in New Zealand. See paragraph 4 of Article 22 (Relief from Double Taxation).

For purposes of the saving clause, "residence" is determined under Article 4 (Residence). Thus, an individual who is a resident of the United States under the Code (but not a U.S. citizen) but who is determined to be a resident of New Zealand under the tie-breaker rules of Article 4 would be subject to U.S. tax only to the extent permitted by the Convention. The United States would not be permitted to apply its statutory rules to that person to the extent the rules are inconsistent with the treaty.

However, the person would be treated as a U.S. resident for U.S. tax purposes other than determining the individual's U.S. tax liability. For example, in determining under Code section 957 whether a foreign corporation is a controlled foreign corporation, shares in that corporation held by the individual would be considered to be held by a U.S. resident. As a result, other U.S. citizens or residents might be deemed to be United States shareholders of a controlled foreign corporation subject to current inclusion of Subpart F income recognized by the corporation. See Treas. Reg. section 301.7701(b)-7(a)(3).

Under paragraph 3, the United States also reserves its right to tax former citizens and former long-term residents for a period of ten years following the loss of such status with respect to income from sources within the United States (including income deemed under the domestic law of the United States to arise from such sources). Thus, paragraph 3 allows the United States to tax former U.S. citizens and former U.S. long-term residents in accordance with section 877 of the Code. Section 877 generally applies to a former citizen or long-term resident of the United States who relinquishes citizenship or terminates long-term residency before June 17, 2008, if he fails to certify that he has complied with U.S. tax laws during the 5 preceding years, or if either of the following criteria exceed established thresholds: (a) the average annual net income tax of such individual for the period of 5 taxable years ending before the date of the loss of status, or (b) the net worth of such individual as of the date of the loss of status. The thresholds for the average annual net income tax are adjusted annually for inflation. The United States defines "long-term resident" as an individual (other than a U.S. citizen) who is a lawful permanent resident of the United States in at least 8 of the prior 15 taxable years. An individual is not treated as a lawful permanent resident for any taxable year if such individual is treated as a resident of a foreign country under the provisions of a tax treaty between the United States and the foreign country and the individual does not waive the benefits of such treaty applicable to residents of the foreign country.

Paragraph 2

Paragraph 2 amends Article I of the existing Convention by adding new paragraphs 5 and 6.

New paragraph 5 specifically relates to non-discrimination obligations of the Contracting States under the General Agreement on Trade in Services (the "GATS"). The provisions of paragraph 5 are an exception to the rule provided in paragraph 2 of this Article under which the Convention shall not restrict in any manner any benefit now or hereafter accorded by any other agreement between the Contracting States.

Subparagraph 5(a) provides that, unless the competent authorities determine that a taxation measure is not within the scope of the Convention, the national treatment obligations of the GATS shall not apply with respect to that measure. Further, any question arising as to the interpretation of the Convention, including in particular whether a measure is within the scope of the Convention shall be considered only by the competent authorities of the Contracting States, and the procedures under the Convention exclusively shall apply to the dispute. Thus, paragraph 3 of Article XXII (Consultation) of the GATS may not be used to bring a dispute before the World Trade Organization unless the competent authorities of both Contracting States have determined that the relevant taxation measure is not within the scope of Article 23 (Non-Discrimination) of the Convention.

The term "measure" for these purposes is defined broadly in subparagraph 5(b). It would include, for example, a law, regulation, rule, procedure, decision, administrative action or guidance, or any other form of measure.

New paragraph 6 addresses special issues presented by fiscally transparent entities such as partnerships and certain estates and trusts. Because countries may take different views as to when an entity is fiscally transparent, the risk of both double taxation and double non-taxation is relatively high. The intention of paragraph 6 is to eliminate a number of technical problems that arguably would have prevented investors using such entities from claiming treaty benefits, even though such investors would be subject to tax on the income derived through such entities. The provision also prevents the use of such entities to claim treaty benefits in circumstances where the person investing through such an entity is not subject to tax on the income in its State of residence. The provision, and the corresponding requirements of the substantive rules of Articles 6 (Income from Real Property) through 15 (Dependent Personal Services) and 17 (Artistes and Athletes) through 21 (Other Income), should be read with those two goals in mind.

In general, paragraph 6 relates to entities that are not subject to tax at the entity level, as distinct from entities that are subject to tax, but with respect to which tax may be relieved under an integrated system. This paragraph applies to any resident of a Contracting State who is entitled to income derived through an entity that is treated as fiscally transparent under the laws of either Contracting State. Entities falling under this description in the United States include partnerships, common investment trusts under section 584 of the Code, and grantor trusts. This paragraph also applies to U.S. limited liability companies ("LLCs") that are treated as partnerships or as disregarded entities for U.S. tax purposes.

Under paragraph 6, an item of income derived by such a fiscally transparent entity will be considered to be derived by a resident of a Contracting State if a resident is treated under the taxation laws of that State as deriving the item of income. For example, if a company that is a resident of New Zealand pays interest to an entity that is treated as fiscally transparent for U.S. tax purposes, the interest will be considered derived by a resident of the United States only to the extent that the taxation laws of the United States treats one or more U.S. residents (whose status as U.S. residents is determined, for this purpose, under U.S. tax law) as deriving the interest for U.S. tax purposes. In the case of a partnership, the persons who are, under U.S. tax laws, treated as partners of the entity would normally be the persons whom the U.S. tax laws would treat as deriving the interest income through the partnership. Also, it follows that persons whom the United States treats as partners but who are not U.S. residents for U.S. tax purposes may not claim any benefit under the Convention for the interest paid to the entity, because they are not residents of the United States for purposes of claiming this treaty benefit. If, however, they are treated as residents of a third country under the provisions of an income tax convention which that country has with New Zealand, they may be entitled to claim a benefit under that convention. In contrast, if, for example, an entity is organized under U.S. laws and is classified as a corporation for U.S. tax purposes, interest paid by a company that is a resident of New Zealand to the U.S. entity will be considered derived by a resident of the United States since the U.S. corporation is treated under U.S. taxation laws as a resident of the United States and as deriving the income.

The same result obtains even if the entity were viewed differently under the tax laws of New Zealand (*e.g.*, as not fiscally transparent in the first example above where the entity is treated as a partnership for U.S. tax purposes). Similarly, the characterization of the entity in a third country is also irrelevant, even if the entity is organized in that third country. The results follow regardless of whether the entity is disregarded as a separate entity under the laws of one jurisdiction but not the other, such as a single owner entity that is viewed as a branch for U.S. tax purposes and as a corporation for tax purposes under the laws of New Zealand. These results also obtain regardless of where the entity is organized (*i.e.*, in the United States, in New Zealand or, as noted above, in a third country).

For example, income from U.S. sources received by an entity organized under the laws of the United States, which is treated for tax purposes under the laws of New Zealand as a corporation and is owned by a shareholder who is a resident of New Zealand for its tax purposes, is not considered derived by the shareholder of that corporation even if, under the tax laws of the United States, the entity is treated as fiscally transparent. Rather, for purposes of the treaty, the income is treated as derived by the U.S. entity.

These principles also apply to trusts to the extent that they are fiscally transparent in either Contracting State. For example, if X, a resident of New Zealand, creates a revocable trust in the United States and names persons resident in a third country as the beneficiaries of the trust, the trust's income would be regarded as being derived by a resident of New Zealand only to the extent that the laws of New Zealand treat X as deriving the income for its tax purposes, perhaps through application of rules similar to the U.S. "grantor trust" rules.

As another example, assume income from U.S. sources is received by a New Zealand accumulation trust created by a New Zealand resident settlor, with a NZ trustee, and one New Zealand beneficiary and one third-country beneficiary. For New Zealand tax purposes, the trustee is viewed as liable for tax because the income is being accumulated in the trust. Therefore, the trustee, as the legal owner of the income, is considered as deriving the income for purposes of applying the Convention.

Paragraph 6 is not an exception to the saving clause of paragraph 3. Accordingly, paragraph 6 does not prevent a Contracting State from taxing an entity that is treated as a resident of that State under its tax law. For example, if a U.S. LLC with members who are residents of New Zealand elects to be taxed as a corporation for U.S. tax purposes, the United States will tax that LLC on its worldwide income on a net basis, without regard to whether New Zealand views the LLC as fiscally transparent.

ARTICLE II

Article II of the Protocol replaces Article 2 (Taxes Covered) of the existing Convention. Article 2 specifies the U.S. taxes and the taxes of New Zealand to which the Convention applies. With two exceptions, the taxes specified in Article 2 are the covered taxes for all purposes of the Convention. A broader coverage applies, however, for purposes of Articles 23 (Non-Discrimination) and 25 (Exchange of Information and Administrative Assistance). Article 23 applies with respect to all taxes, including those imposed by state and local governments. Article 25 (Exchange of Information and Administrative Assistance) applies with respect to all taxes imposed at the national level.

Paragraph 1 of Article 2

Paragraph 1 identifies the category of taxes to which the Convention applies. Paragraph 1 is based on the U.S. and OECD Models and defines the scope of application of the Convention. The Convention applies to taxes on income, including gains, imposed on behalf of a Contracting State, irrespective of the manner in which they are levied. Except with respect to Article 23, state and local taxes are not covered by the Convention.

Paragraph 2 of Article 2

Paragraph 2 also is based on the U.S. and OECD Models and provides a definition of taxes on income and on capital gains. The Convention covers taxes on total income or any part of income and includes tax on gains derived from the alienation of property. The Convention does not apply, however, to social security charges, or any other charges where there is a direct connection between the levy and individual benefits. Nor does it apply to property taxes, except with respect to Article 23.

Paragraph 3 of Article 2

Paragraph 3 lists the taxes in force at the time of signature of the Convention to which the Convention applies.

The existing covered taxes of New Zealand are identified in subparagraph 3(a), as the income tax.

Subparagraph 3(b) provides that the existing U.S. taxes subject to the rules of the Convention are the Federal income taxes imposed by the Code, together with the excise taxes imposed with respect to the investment income of foreign private foundations (Code section 4940). Social security and unemployment taxes (Code sections 1401, 3101, 3111 and 3301) are excluded from coverage.

Paragraph 4 of Article 2

Paragraph 4 is in all material respects the same as paragraph 2 of Article 2 of the existing Convention. Under paragraph 4, the Convention will apply to any taxes that are identical, or substantially similar, to those enumerated in paragraph 3, and which are imposed in addition to, or in place of, the existing taxes after December 1, 2008, the date of signature of the Protocol. The paragraph also provides that the competent authorities of the Contracting States will notify each other of any changes that have been made in their laws, whether tax laws or non-tax laws, that significantly affect their obligations under the Convention. Non-tax laws that may affect a Contracting State's obligations under the Convention may include, for example, laws affecting bank secrecy.

ARTICLE III

Article III of the Protocol amends Article 3 (General Definitions) of the existing Convention.

Paragraph 1

Paragraph 1 of the Protocol amends subparagraph 1(b) of Article 3 of the existing Convention by including a new definition of the term "company." The term "company" is defined in subparagraph 1(b) as a body corporate or an entity treated as a body corporate for tax purposes in the state where it is organized. The definition refers to the law of the state in which an entity is organized in order to ensure that an entity that is treated as fiscally transparent in its country of residence will not get inappropriate benefits, such as the reduced withholding rate provided by subparagraph 2(b) of Article 10 (Dividends). It also ensures that the Limitation on Benefits provisions of Article 16 will be applied at the appropriate level.

Paragraph 2

Paragraph 2 of the Protocol replaces subparagraph 1(d) of Article 3 of the existing Convention by defining the terms "enterprise of a Contracting State" and "enterprise of the other Contracting State" as an enterprise carried on by a resident of a Contracting State and an enterprise carried on by a resident of the other Contracting State. An enterprise of a Contracting State need not be carried on in that State. It may be carried on in the other Contracting State or a third state (e.g., a U.S. corporation doing all of its business in New Zealand would still be a U.S. enterprise).

These terms also encompass an enterprise conducted through an entity (such as a partnership) that is treated as fiscally transparent in the Contracting State where the entity's owner is resident. In accordance with Article 4 (Resident), entities that are fiscally transparent in the Contracting State in which their owners are resident are not considered to be residents of that Contracting State (although income derived by such entities may be taxed as the income of a resident, if taxed in the hands of resident partners or other owners). An enterprise conducted by such an entity will be treated as carried on by a resident of a Contracting State to the extent its partners or other owners are residents. This approach is consistent with the Code, which under section 875 attributes a trade or business conducted by a partnership to its partners and a trade or business conducted by an estate or trust to its beneficiaries.

Paragraph 3

Paragraph 3 of the Protocol replaces paragraph 1(g) of Article 3 of the existing Convention. Paragraph 3 of the Protocol sets out the geographical scope of the Convention with respect to the United States. It encompasses the United States of America, including the states, the District of Columbia and the territorial sea of the United States. The term does not include Puerto Rico, the United States Virgin Islands, Guam the Commonwealth of the Northern Mariana Islands or any other U.S. possession or territory. For certain purposes, the term "United States" includes the sea bed and subsoil of undersea areas adjacent to the territorial sea of the United States. This extension applies to the extent that the United States exercises sovereignty in accordance with international law for the purpose of natural resource exploration and exploitation of such areas. This extension of the definition applies, however, only if the person, property or activity to which the Convention is being applied is connected with such natural resource exploration or exploitation. Thus, it would not include any activity involving the sea floor of an area over which the United States exercised sovereignty for natural resource purposes if that activity was unrelated to the exploration and exploitation of natural resources. This result is consistent with the result that would be obtained under Code section 638, which treats the continental shelf as part of the United States for purposes of natural resource exploration and exploitation.

Paragraph 4

Paragraph 4 of the Protocol replaces paragraph 1(h) of Article 3 of the existing Convention. Paragraph 4 of the Protocol sets out the geographical scope of the Convention with respect to New Zealand. The term "New Zealand" encompasses the territory of New Zealand but does not include Tokelau; it also includes any area beyond the territorial sea designated under New Zealand legislation and in accordance with international law as an area in which New Zealand may exercise sovereign rights with respect to natural resources.

Paragraph 5

Paragraph 5 of the Protocol amends paragraph 1(j) of Article 3 of the existing Convention by deleting the final period and replacing it with a comma.

Paragraph 6

Paragraph 6 of the Protocol amends paragraph 1 of Article 3 of the existing Convention by adding four new subparagraphs (k), (l), (m), and (n) to paragraph 1 of Article 3 of the existing Convention.

Subparagraph 1(k) defines the term "national," as it relates to the United States and to New Zealand. This term is relevant for purposes of Articles 19 (Government Service) and 23 (Non-Discrimination). A national of one of the Contracting States is (1) an individual who is a citizen of that State, and (2) any legal person, partnership or association deriving its status, as such, from the law in force in the State where it is established.

Subparagraph (l) defines the term "pension fund" to include any person established in a Contracting State that is operated principally to administer or provide pension or retirement benefits or to earn income for the benefit of one or more such arrangements and in the case of the United States is generally exempt from income taxation. In the case of New Zealand, the term refers to a superannuation scheme registered under the Superannuation Schemes Act 1989, a KiwiSaver Scheme registered under the KiwiSaver Act 2006, the New Zealand Superannuation Fund, or the Government Superannuation Fund.

For application of the Convention by the United States, the term "pension fund" includes the following: a trust providing pension or retirement benefits under a Code section 401(a) qualified pension plan, profit sharing or stock bonus plan, a Code section 403(a) qualified annuity plan, a Code section 403(b) plan, a trust that is an individual retirement account under Code section 408, a Roth individual retirement account under Code section 408A, or a simple retirement account under Code section 408(p), a trust providing pension or retirement benefits under a simplified employee pension plan under Code section 408(k), a trust described in section 457(g) providing pension or retirement benefits under a Code section 457(b) plan, and the Thrift Savings Fund (section 7701(j)). Section 401(k) plans and group trusts described in Rev. Rul. 81-100, 1981-1 C.B. 326, and meeting the conditions of Rev. Rul. 2004-67, 2204-2 C.B. 28, qualify as pension funds to the extent they are covered by Code section 401(a) plans and other pension funds.

Subparagraph (m) defines the term "enterprise" as any activity or set of activities that constitutes the carrying on of a business. The term "business" is not defined, but subparagraph (n) provides that it includes the performance of professional services and other activities of an independent character. The introduction of this definition is necessary in connection with the deletion of Article 14 (Independent Personal Services) as provided in Article X of the Protocol. Both subparagraphs are identical to definitions recently added to the OECD Model in connection with the deletion of Article 14 from the OECD Model. The inclusion of the two definitions in subparagraph (m) and (n) is intended to clarify that income from the performance of professional services or other activities of an independent character is dealt with under Article 7 (Business Profits) and not Article 21 (Other Income).

Paragraph 7

Paragraph 7 of the Protocol replaces paragraph 3 of Article 3 of the existing Convention and addresses the terms that are not defined in the Convention.

New paragraph 3 of Article 3 provides that in the application of the Convention, any term used but not defined in the Convention will have the meaning that it has under the law of the Contracting State whose tax is being applied, unless the context requires otherwise, or the competent authorities have agreed on a different meaning pursuant to Article 24 (Mutual Agreement Procedure). If the term is defined under both the tax and non-tax laws of a Contracting State, the definition in the tax law will take precedence over the definition in the non-tax laws. Finally, there also may be cases where the tax laws of a State contain multiple definitions of the same term. In such a case, the definition used for purposes of the particular provision at issue, if any, should be used.

If the meaning of a term cannot be readily determined under the law of a Contracting State, or if there is a conflict in meaning under the laws of the two States that creates difficulties in the application of the Convention, the competent authorities, as indicated in paragraph 3(f) of Article 24, may establish a common meaning in order to prevent double taxation or to further any other purpose of the Convention. This common meaning need not conform to the meaning of the term under the laws of either Contracting State.

The reference in new paragraph 3 to the internal law of a Contracting State means the law in effect at the time the Convention is being applied, not the law as in effect at the time the Convention was signed. The use of "ambulatory" definitions, however, may lead to results that are at variance with the intentions of the negotiators and of the Contracting States when the Convention was negotiated and ratified. The reference in both paragraphs 1 and 3 of the Convention to the "context otherwise requir[ing]" a definition different from the Convention definition, in paragraph 1, or from the internal law definition of the Contracting State whose tax is being imposed, under paragraph 3, refers to a circumstance where the result intended by the Contracting States is different from the result that would obtain under either the paragraph 1 definition or the statutory definition. Thus, flexibility in defining terms is necessary and permitted.

ARTICLE IV

Paragraph 1

Paragraph 1 of Article IV of the Protocol replaces paragraph 1 of Article 4 (Residence) of the existing Convention. The term "resident of a Contracting State" is defined in paragraph 1. In general, this definition incorporates the definitions of residence in U.S. law and that of New Zealand by referring to a resident as a person who, under the laws of a Contracting State, is subject to tax there by reason of his domicile, residence, citizenship, place of management, place of incorporation or any other similar criterion. Thus, residents of the United States include aliens who are considered U.S. residents under Code section 7701(b). Paragraph 1 also specifically includes the two Contracting States, and political subdivisions and local authorities of the two States, as residents for purposes of the Convention.

Certain entities that are nominally subject to tax but that in practice are rarely required to pay tax also would generally be treated as residents and therefore accorded treaty benefits. For example, a U.S. Regulated Investment Company (RIC) and a U.S. Real Estate Investment Trust (REIT) are residents of the United States for purposes of the Convention. Although the income earned by these entities normally is not subject to U.S. tax in the hands of the entity, they are taxable to the extent that they do not currently distribute their profits, and therefore may be regarded as "liable to tax." They also must satisfy a number of requirements under the Code in order to be entitled to special tax treatment.

Under paragraph 1 of Article 4 of the Convention, a person who is liable to tax in a Contracting State only in respect of income from sources within that State or of profits attributable to a permanent establishment in that State will not be treated as a resident of that Contracting State for purposes of the Convention. Thus, a consular official of New Zealand who is posted in the United States, who may be subject to U.S. tax on U.S. source investment income, but is not taxable in the United States on non-U.S. source income (see Code section 7701(b)(5)(B)), would not be considered a resident of the United States for purposes of the Convention. Similarly, an enterprise of New Zealand with a permanent establishment in the United States is not, by virtue of that permanent establishment, a resident of the United States. The enterprise generally is subject to U.S. tax only with respect to its income that is attributable to the U.S. permanent establishment, not with respect to its worldwide income, as it would be if it were a U.S. resident.

Paragraph 2

Paragraph 2 amends subparagraph 2(c) of Article 4 of the existing Convention by deleting the word "citizen" and replacing it with the word "national."

Paragraph 3

Paragraph 3 amends subparagraph 2(d) of Article 4 of the existing Convention by deleting the word "citizen" and replacing it with the word "national."

Paragraph 4

Paragraph 4 amends paragraph 4 of Article 4 of the existing Convention by deleting the words "shall be treated as a resident of neither Contracting State for purposes of the Convention" and replacing them with the words "will not be treated as a resident of either Contracting Stated for purposes of its claiming any benefits provided by the Convention."

Dual residents other than individuals (such as companies, trusts, or estates) are addressed by paragraph 4. If such a person is, under the rules of paragraph 1 or 2, resident in both Contracting States, the competent authorities shall seek to determine a single State of residence for that person for purposes of the Convention. If the competent authorities do not reach an agreement on a single State of residence, that dual resident may not claim any benefit accorded to residents of a Contracting State by the Convention. The dual resident may, however, claim any benefits that are not limited to residents, such as those provided by paragraph 1 of Article 23 (Non-Discrimination). Thus, for example, a State cannot impose discriminatory taxation on a dual resident company.

Dual residents also may be treated as a resident of a Contracting State for purposes other than that of obtaining benefits under the Convention. For example, if a dual resident company pays a dividend to a resident of New Zealand, the U.S. paying agent would withhold on that dividend at the appropriate treaty rate because reduced withholding is a benefit enjoyed by the resident of New Zealand, not by the dual resident company. The dual resident company that paid the dividend would, for this purpose, be treated as a resident of the United States under the Convention. In addition, information relating to dual residents can be exchanged under the Convention because, by its terms, Article 25 (Exchange of Information and Administrative Assistance) is not limited to residents of the Contracting States.

ARTICLE V

Article V of the Protocol amends Article 7 (Business Profits) of the existing Convention by adding new paragraphs 8 and 9.

New paragraph 8 incorporates into the existing Convention the rule of Code section 864(c)(6). Like the Code section on which it is based, paragraph 8 provides that any income or gain attributable to a permanent establishment during its existence is taxable in the Contracting State where the permanent establishment is situated, even if the payment of that income or gain is deferred until after the permanent establishment ceases to exist. This rule applies with respect to paragraphs 1 and 2 of Article 7, paragraph 6 of Article 10 (Dividends), paragraph 4 of Article 11 (Interest), paragraph 4 of Articles 12 (Royalties) and paragraph 6 of Article 13 (Capital Gains).

The effect of this rule can be illustrated by the following example. Assume a company that is a resident of New Zealand and that maintains a permanent establishment in the United States winds up the permanent establishment's business and sells the permanent establishment's inventory and assets to a U.S. buyer at the end of year 1 in exchange for an interest-bearing installment obligation payable in full at the end of year 3. Despite the fact that Article 13's threshold requirement for U.S. taxation is not met in year 3 because the company has no permanent establishment in the United States, the United States may tax the deferred income payment recognized by the company in year 3.

New paragraph 9 clarifies the treatment of fiscally transparent entities (including trusts) and beneficial owners thereof under Article 7 of the Convention. New Zealand requested this clarification because, under New Zealand law, the trustees of a trust, as the legal owner of the trust property, might be regarded as the only person having a permanent establishment (rather than the beneficiaries of the trust, who have a beneficial entitlement to the income but no legal ownership). Thus, absent this clarification, any permanent establishment resulting from that trade or business might be considered to be that of the trustees, rather than that of the beneficiaries.

New paragraph 9 provides that if a fiscally transparent entity (or trustee) has a permanent establishment in a Contracting State and a resident of the other Contracting State is beneficially entitled to a share of the business profits from the business that is carried on by the fiscally transparent entity (or trustee) through that permanent establishment, then the beneficial owner is treated as carrying on a business through a permanent establishment in that Contracting State, and its share of business profits therefrom are attributed to the permanent establishment. Thus, if a trust with a U.S. beneficiary carries on a business in New Zealand through its trustee, and that trustee's actions rise to the level of a permanent establishment, then the U.S. beneficiary will be treated as having a permanent establishment in New Zealand and the profits of the trust associated with that permanent establishment will be treated as business profits under Article 7. Since paragraph 9 is added solely to address the New Zealand law relating to trusts, the absence of similar language in other U.S. tax treaties should not be read as implying that a resident may avoid permanent establishment treatment and business profits by investing through a fiscally transparent entity.

ARTICLE VI

Article VI of the Protocol replaces Article 10 (Dividends) of the existing Convention. Article 10, provides rules for the taxation of dividends paid by a company that is a resident of one Contracting State to a beneficial owner that is a resident of the other Contracting State. The Article provides for full residence country taxation of such dividends and a limited source-State right to tax. Article 10, as amended by the Protocol, also provides rules for the imposition of a tax on branch profits by the State of source. Finally, the Article prohibits a State from imposing taxes on a company resident in the other Contracting State, other than a branch profits tax, on undistributed earnings.

Paragraph 1 of Article 10

Paragraph 1 is in all material respects the same as paragraph 1 of Article 10 of the existing Convention. The right of a shareholder's country of residence to tax dividends arising in the source country is preserved by paragraph 1, which permits a Contracting State to tax its residents on dividends paid to them by a company that is a resident of the other Contracting State. For dividends from any other source paid to a resident, Article 20 (Other Income) grants the State of residence exclusive taxing jurisdiction (other than for dividends attributable to a permanent establishment in the other State).

Paragraph 2 of Article 10

The State of source also may tax dividends beneficially owned by a resident of the other State, subject to the limitations of paragraphs 2 and 3. Paragraph 2 generally limits the rate of withholding tax in the State of source on dividends paid by a company resident in that State to 15 percent of the gross amount of the dividend. If, however, the beneficial owner of the dividend is a company resident in the other State and owns directly shares representing at least 10 percent of the voting power of the company paying the dividend, then the rate of withholding tax in the State of source is limited to 5 percent of the gross amount of the dividend. For purposes of the application of paragraph 2, the term "voting power" refers to the voting stock in a company. Shares are considered voting shares if they provide the power to elect, appoint or replace any person vested with the powers ordinarily exercised by the board of directors of a U.S. corporation.

The benefits of paragraph 2 may be granted at the time of payment by means of reduced rate of withholding tax at source. It also is consistent with the paragraph for tax to be withheld at the time of payment at full statutory rates, and the treaty benefit to be granted by means of a subsequent refund so long as such procedures are applied in a reasonable manner.

The determination of whether the ownership threshold for subparagraph 2(a) is met for purposes of the 5 percent maximum rate of withholding tax is made on the date on which entitlement to the dividend is determined. Thus, in the case of a dividend from a U.S. company, the determination of whether the ownership threshold is met generally would be made on the dividend record date.

Paragraph 2 does not affect the taxation of the profits out of which the dividends are paid. The taxation by a Contracting State of the income of its resident companies is governed by the internal law of the Contracting State, subject to the provisions of paragraph 4 of Article 23 (Non-Discrimination).

The term "beneficial owner" is not defined in the Convention, and is, therefore, defined as under the internal law of the State granting treaty benefits (*i.e.*, the source country). The beneficial owner of the dividend for purposes of Article 10 is the person to which the dividend income is attributable for tax purposes under the laws of the source State. Thus, if a dividend paid by a corporation that is a resident of one of the States (as determined under Article 4 (Resident)) is received by a nominee or agent that is a resident of the other State on behalf of a person that is not a resident of that other State, the dividend is not entitled to the benefits of this Article. However, a dividend received by a nominee on behalf of a resident of that other State would be entitled to benefits. These limitations are confirmed by paragraph 12 of the Commentary to Article 10 of the OECD Model.

Special rules, however, apply to shares that are held through fiscally transparent entities. In that case, the rules of paragraph 6 of Article 1 (General Scope) will apply to determine whether the dividends should be treated as having been derived by a resident of a Contracting State. Residence State principles shall be used to determine who derives the dividend, to assure that the dividends for which the source State grants benefits of the Convention will be taken into account for tax purposes by a resident of the residence State. Source state principles of beneficial ownership shall then apply to determine whether the person who derives the dividends, or another resident of the other Contracting State, is the beneficial owner of the dividend. The source State may conclude that the person who derives the dividend in the residence State is a mere nominee, agent, conduit, etc., for a third country resident and deny benefits of the Convention. If the person who derives the dividend under paragraph 6 of Article 1 would not be treated under the source State's principles for determining beneficial ownership as a nominee, agent, custodian, conduit, etc., that person will be treated as the beneficial owner of the income, profits or gains for purposes of the Convention.

Assume, for instance, that a company resident in New Zealand pays a dividend to LLC, an entity which is treated as fiscally transparent for U.S. tax purposes but is treated as a company for New Zealand tax purposes. USCo, a company incorporated in the United States, is the sole interest holder in LLC. Paragraph 6 of Article 1 provides that USCo derives the dividend. New Zealand's principles of beneficial ownership shall then be applied to USCo. If under the laws of New Zealand USCo is found not to be the beneficial owner of the dividend, USCo will not be entitled to the benefits of Article 10 with respect to such dividend. The payment may be entitled to benefits, however, if USCo is found to be a nominee, agent, custodian or conduit for a person who is a resident of the United States.

Beyond identifying the person to whom the principles of beneficial ownership shall be applied, the principles of paragraph 6 of Article 1 will also apply when determining whether other requirements, such as the ownership threshold of subparagraph 2(a) have been satisfied.

For example, assume that NZCo, a company that is a resident of New Zealand, owns all of the outstanding shares in ThirdDE, an entity that is disregarded for U.S. tax purposes and that is resident in a third country. ThirdDE owns 100 percent of the stock of USCo. New Zealand views ThirdDE as fiscally transparent under its domestic law, and taxes NZCo currently on the income derived by ThirdDE. In this case, NZCo is treated as deriving the dividends paid by USCo under paragraph 6 of Article 1. Moreover, NZCo is treated as owning the shares of USCo directly. The Convention does not address what constitutes direct ownership for purposes of Article 10. As a result, whether ownership is direct is determined under the internal law of the State granting treaty benefits (*i.e.*, the source country) unless the context otherwise requires. Accordingly, a company that holds stock through such an entity will generally be considered to directly own such stock for purposes of Article 10.

This result may change, however, if ThirdDE is regarded as non-fiscally transparent under the laws of New Zealand. Assuming that ThirdDE is treated as non-fiscally transparent by New Zealand, the income will not be treated as derived by a resident of New Zealand for purposes of the Convention. However, ThirdDE may still be entitled to the benefits of the U.S. tax treaty, if any, with its country of residence.

The same principles would apply in determining whether companies holding shares through fiscally transparent entities such as partnerships, trusts, and estates would qualify for benefits. As a result, companies holding shares through such entities may be able to claim the benefits of subparagraph (a) under certain circumstances. The lower rate applies when the company's proportionate share of the shares held by the intermediate entity meets the 10 percent threshold, and the company meets the requirements of Article 1(6) (*i.e.*, the company's country of residence treats the intermediate entity as fiscally transparent) with respect to the dividend. Whether this ownership threshold is satisfied may be difficult to determine and often will require an analysis of the partnership or trust agreement.

Paragraph 3

Paragraph 3 provides for exclusive residence country taxation of dividends (*i.e.*, an elimination of withholding tax) with respect to certain dividends distributed by a company resident in one Contracting State to a company resident in the other Contracting State. As described further below, this elimination of withholding tax is available with respect to certain inter-company dividends.

Subparagraph 3(a) provides for the elimination of withholding tax on dividends beneficially owned by a company that has owned 80 percent or more of the voting power of the company paying the dividend for the 12-month period ending on the date entitlement to the dividend is determined. The determination of whether the beneficial owner of the dividends owns at least 80 percent of the voting power of the paying company is made by taking into account stock owned both directly and indirectly through one or more residents of either Contracting State.

Eligibility for the elimination of withholding tax provided by subparagraph (a) is subject to additional restrictions based on, and supplementing, the rules of Article 16 (Limitation of Benefits). Accordingly, a company that meets the holding requirements described above will qualify for the benefits of paragraph 3 only if it also: (1) meets the "publicly traded" test of subparagraph 2(c) of Article 16, (2) meets the "ownership-base erosion" and "active trade or business" tests described in clause (i) and (ii) of subparagraph 2(e) and paragraph 3 of Article 16, or (3) is granted the benefits of paragraph 3 of Article 10 by the competent authority of the source State pursuant to paragraph 4 of Article 16.

These restrictions are necessary because of the increased pressure on the limitation of benefits tests resulting from the fact that the United States has relatively few treaties that provide for such elimination of withholding tax on inter-company dividends. The additional restrictions are intended to prevent companies from reorganizing in order to become eligible for the elimination of withholding tax in circumstances where the limitation of benefits provision does not provide sufficient protection against treaty shopping.

For example, assume that ThirdCo is a company resident in a third country that does not have a tax treaty with the United States providing for the elimination of withholding tax on inter-company dividends. ThirdCo owns directly 100 percent of the issued and outstanding voting stock of USCo, a U.S. company, and of NZCo, a New Zealand company. NZCo is a substantial company that manufactures widgets; USCo distributes those widgets in the United States. If ThirdCo contributes to NZCo all the stock of USCo, dividends paid by USCo to NZCo would qualify for treaty benefits under the active trade or business test of paragraph 3 of Article 16. However, allowing ThirdCo to qualify for the elimination of withholding tax, which is not available to it under the third state's treaty with the United States (if any), would encourage treaty-shopping.

In order to prevent this type of treaty shopping, paragraph 3(b) of Article 10 requires NZCo to meet the ownership-base erosion requirements of clause (i) and (ii) of subparagraph 2(e) of Article 16, in addition to the active trade or business test of paragraph 3 of Article 16. Thus, NZCo would not qualify for the exemption from withholding tax unless (i) on at least half the days of the taxable year, at least 50 percent of each class of its shares was owned by persons that are residents of New Zealand and eligible for treaty benefits under certain specified tests and (ii) less than 50 percent of NZCo's gross income is paid in deductible payments to persons that are not residents of either Contracting State eligible for benefits under those specified tests. Because NZCo is wholly owned by a third country resident, NZCo could not qualify for the elimination of withholding tax on dividends from USCo under the ownership-base erosion test and the active trade or business test. Consequently, NZCo would need to qualify under another test or obtain discretionary relief from the competent authority under Article 16(4). For purposes of Article 10(3)(b), it is not sufficient for a company to qualify for treaty benefits generally under the active trade or business test or the ownership-base erosion test unless it qualifies for treaty benefits under both.

Alternatively, companies that are publicly traded or subsidiaries of publicly-traded companies will generally qualify for the elimination of withholding tax under subparagraph 3(a) of Article 10. Thus, a company that is a resident of New Zealand and that meets the requirements of clause (i) or (ii) of subparagraph 2(c) of Article 16, as amended by the Protocol, will be entitled to the elimination of withholding tax, subject to the 12-month holding period requirement of Article 10(3).

If a company does not qualify for the elimination of withholding tax under any of the foregoing objective tests, it may request a determination from the relevant competent authority pursuant to paragraph 4 of Article 16. Benefits may be granted with respect to an item of income if the competent authority of the Contracting State in which the income arises determines that the establishment, acquisition or maintenance of such resident and the conduct of its operations did not have as one of its principal purposes the obtaining of benefits under the Convention.

Paragraph 4 of Article 10

Paragraph 4 imposes limitations on the rate reductions provided by paragraphs 2 and 3 in the case of dividends paid by a RIC or a REIT.

The first sentence of subparagraph 4(a) provides that dividends paid by a RIC or a REIT are not eligible for the 5 percent rate of withholding tax of subparagraph 2(a) or the elimination of withholding tax of paragraph 3.

The second sentence of subparagraph 4(a) provides that the 15 percent maximum rate of withholding tax of subparagraph 2(b) applies to dividends paid by RICs.

The third sentence of subparagraph 4(a) provides that the 15 percent rate of withholding tax also applies to dividends paid by a REIT provided that one of the three following conditions is met. First, the beneficial owner of the dividend is an individual or a pension fund, in either case holding an interest of not more than 10 percent in the REIT. Second, the dividend is paid with respect to a class of stock that is publicly traded and the beneficial owner of the dividend is a person holding an interest of not more than 5 percent of any class of the REIT's shares. Third, the beneficial owner of the dividend holds an interest in the REIT of not more than 10 percent and the REIT is "diversified." Subparagraph 4(b) provides that a REIT is diversified if the gross value of no single interest in real property held by the REIT exceeds 10 percent of the gross value of the REIT's total interest in real property. Foreclosure property is not considered an interest in real property, and a REIT holding a partnership interest is treated as owning its proportionate share of any interest in real property held by the partnership.

The restrictions set out above are intended to prevent the use of these entities to gain inappropriate U.S. tax benefits. For example, a company resident in New Zealand that wishes to hold a diversified portfolio of U.S. corporate shares could hold the portfolio directly and would bear a U.S. withholding tax of 15 percent on all of the dividends that it receives. Alternatively, it could hold the same diversified portfolio by purchasing 10 percent or more of the interests in a RIC that in turn held the portfolio. Absent the special rule in paragraph 4, such use of the RIC could transform portfolio dividends, taxable in the United States under the Convention at a 15 percent maximum rate of withholding tax, into direct investment dividends taxable at a 5 percent maximum rate of withholding tax or eligible for the elimination of source-country withholding tax on dividends as provided in paragraph 3.

Similarly, a resident of New Zealand directly holding U.S. real property would pay U.S. tax upon the sale of the property either at a 30 percent rate of withholding tax on the gross income or at graduated rates on the net income. As in the preceding example, by placing the real property in a REIT, the investor could, absent a special rule, transform income from the sale of real estate into dividend income from the REIT, taxable at the rates provided in Article 10, significantly reducing the U.S. tax that otherwise would be imposed. Paragraph 4 prevents this result and thereby avoids a disparity between the taxation of direct real estate investments and real estate investments made through REIT conduits. In the cases in which paragraph 4 allows a dividend from a REIT to be eligible for the 15 percent rate of withholding tax, the holding in the REIT is not considered the equivalent of a direct holding in the underlying real property.

Paragraph 5 of Article 10

Paragraph 5 defines the term dividends broadly and flexibly. The definition is intended to cover all arrangements that yield a return on an equity investment in a corporation as determined under the tax law of the state of source, as well as arrangements that might be developed in the future.

The term includes income from shares, or other corporate rights that are not treated as debt under the law of the source State, that participate in the profits of the company. The term also includes income that is subjected to the same tax treatment as income from shares by the law of the State of source. Thus, a constructive dividend that results from a non-arm's length transaction between a corporation and a related party is a dividend. In the case of the United States the term dividend includes amounts treated as a dividend under U.S. law upon the sale or redemption of shares or upon a transfer of shares in a reorganization. See, e.g., Rev. Rul. 92-85, 1992-2 C.B. 69 (sale of foreign subsidiary's stock to U.S. sister company is a deemed dividend to extent of the subsidiary's and sister company's earnings and profits). Further, a distribution from a U.S. publicly traded limited partnership, which is taxed as a corporation under U.S. law, is a dividend for purposes of Article 10. However, a distribution by a limited liability company is not taxable by the United States under Article 10, provided the limited liability company is not characterized as an association taxable as a corporation under U.S. law.

New Zealand has certain statutory instruments referred to as "FC1" and "FC2" debentures which correspond to their statutory numbering under The Income Tax Act of 1994. Even though these debentures are debt instruments, New Zealand taxes these instruments as equity and subjects them to their Foreign Investor Tax Credit ("FITC") regime, which provides a mechanism for reducing company tax in respect of profits distributed to non-residents. However, because these debentures are regarded as profit distributions, no deductions are allowed to the company paying them out. The FC1 debentures are debt instruments on which the return is calculated with a reference to profits. The FC2 debentures are debt instruments on which the amount of the debenture is determined by reference to the number of shares the debenture holder holds; thus, the rate is constant but the amount of the debenture fluctuates as it is related to the number of shares. Accordingly, returns from the FC1 and FC2 debentures will be treated as dividends under Article 10.

Finally, a payment denominated as interest that is made by a thinly capitalized corporation may be treated as a dividend to the extent that the debt is recharacterized as equity under the laws of the source State.

Paragraph 6 of Article 10

Paragraph 6 is in all material respects the same as paragraph 3 of Article 10 of the existing Convention. The only change is the deletion of references to "fixed base" and "Article 14 (Independent Personal Services)," to conform to changes made by Article X of the Protocol.

Paragraph 6 provides a rule for taxing dividends paid with respect to holdings that form part of the business property of a permanent establishment. In such case, the rules of Article 7 (Business Profits) shall apply. Accordingly, the dividends will be taxed on a net basis using the rates and rules of taxation generally applicable to residents of the State in which the permanent establishment is located, as such rules may be modified by the Convention. An example of dividends paid with respect to the business property of a permanent establishment would be dividends derived by a dealer in stock or securities from stock or securities that the dealer held for sale to customers.

Paragraph 7 of Article 10

The right of a Contracting State to tax dividends paid by a company that is a resident of the other Contracting State is restricted by paragraph 7 to cases in which the dividends are paid to a resident of that Contracting State or are attributable to a permanent establishment in that Contracting State. Thus, a Contracting State may not impose a "secondary" withholding tax on dividends paid by a nonresident company out of earnings and profits from that Contracting State.

The paragraph also restricts the right of a Contracting State to impose corporate level taxes on undistributed profits, other than a branch profits tax. The paragraph does not restrict a State's right to tax its resident shareholders on undistributed earnings of a corporation resident in the other State. Thus, the authority of the United States to impose taxes on subpart F income and on earnings deemed invested in U.S. property, and its tax on income of a passive foreign investment company that is a qualified electing fund is in no way restricted by this provision.

Paragraph 8 of Article 10

Paragraph 8 permits the United States to impose a branch profits tax on a company resident in New Zealand. The tax is in addition to other taxes permitted by the Convention. The term "company" is defined in subparagraph 1(b) of Article 3 (General Definitions).

The United States may impose a branch profits tax on a New Zealand company if the company has income attributable to a permanent establishment in the United States, derives income from real property in the United States that is taxed on a net basis under Article 6 (Income from Real Property)), or realizes gains taxable in the United States under paragraph 1 of Article 13 (Alienation of Property). In the case of the United States, the imposition of such tax is limited, however, to the portion of the aforementioned items of income that represents the amount of such income that is the "dividend equivalent amount." This is consistent with the relevant rules under the U.S. branch profits tax, and the term dividend equivalent amount is defined under U.S. law. Section 884 of the Code defines the dividend equivalent amount as an amount for a particular year that is equivalent to the income described above that is included in the corporation's effectively connected earnings and profits for that year, after payment of the corporate tax under Article 6, Article 7, or Article 13, reduced for any increase in the branch's U.S. net equity during the year or increased for any reduction in its U.S. net equity during the year. U.S. net equity is U.S. assets less U.S. liabilities. See Treas. Reg. section 1.884-1.

The dividend equivalent amount for any year approximates the dividend that a U.S. branch office would have paid during the year if the branch had been operated as a separate U.S. subsidiary company.

Consistency principles prohibit a taxpayer from applying provisions of the Code and this Convention inconsistently. In the context of the branch profits tax, this consistency requirement means that if a New Zealand company uses the principles of Article 7 to determine its U.S. taxable income, then it must also use those principles to determine its dividend equivalent amount. Similarly, if the New Zealand company instead uses the Code to determine its U.S. taxable income it must also use the Code to determine its dividend equivalent amount. As in the case of Article 7, if a New Zealand company, for example, does not from year to year consistently apply the Code or the Convention to determine its dividend equivalent amount, then the New Zealand company must make appropriate adjustments or recapture amounts that would otherwise be subject to U.S. branch profits tax if it had consistently applied the Code or the Convention to determine its dividend equivalent amount from year to year.

Paragraph 9 of Article 10

Paragraph 9 provides that the tax referred to in paragraph 8, the branch profits tax, shall not be imposed at a rate exceeding the rate specified in subparagraph 2(a), the direct investment dividend withholding rate of five percent. However, this tax shall not be imposed on a company that satisfies either the public trading requirements of clause (i) or (ii) of subparagraph 2(c) of Article 16 (Limitation on Benefits), the ownership and base erosion conditions of clause (i) and (ii) of subparagraph 2(e) of Article 16 provided that the company satisfies the active trade or business test of paragraph 3 of Article 16 with respect to an item of income, profit or gain described in paragraph 8 of the Article, as revised by the Protocol, or that has received a determination by the competent authorities pursuant to paragraph 4 of Article 16.

It is intended that paragraph 9 apply equally if a taxpayer determines its taxable income under the laws of a Contracting State or under the provisions of Article 7. For example, as discussed above in the explanation to paragraph 8, consistency principles require a New Zealand company that determines its U.S. taxable income under the Code to also determine its dividend equivalent amount under the Code. In that case, paragraph 9 would apply even though the New Zealand company did not determine its dividend equivalent amount using the principles of Article 7.

Relationship to Other Articles

Notwithstanding the foregoing limitations on source country taxation of dividends, the saving clause of paragraph 3 of Article 1 (General Scope) permits the United States to tax dividends received by its residents and citizens, subject to the special foreign tax credit rules of paragraph 4 of Article 22 (Relief from Double Taxation), as if the Convention had not come into effect.

The benefits of this Article are also subject to the provisions of Article 16. Thus, if a resident of New Zealand is the beneficial owner of dividends paid by a U.S. corporation, the shareholder must qualify for treaty benefits under at least one of the tests of Article 16 in order to receive the benefits of this Article.

ARTICLE VII

Article VII of the Protocol replaces Article 11 (Interest) of the existing Convention and specifies the taxing jurisdictions over interest arising in one Contracting State and paid to a resident of the other Contracting State.

Paragraph 1 of Article 11

Paragraph 1 is in all material respects the same as paragraph 1 of Article 11 of the existing Convention. Paragraph 1 generally grants to the State of residence the non-exclusive right to tax interest arising in the other Contracting State and paid to its residents.

Paragraph 2 of Article 11

Paragraph 2 is in all material respects the same as paragraph 2 of Article 11 of the existing Convention. Paragraph 2 provides that the State of source also may tax the interest, but if the interest is beneficially owned by a resident of the other Contracting State, the rate of tax will be limited to 10 percent of the gross amount of the interest.

The term "beneficial owner" is not defined in the Convention, and is, therefore, defined under the internal law of the State granting treaty benefits (*i.e.*, the State of source). The beneficial owner of the interest for purposes of Article 11 is the person to which the income is attributable under the laws of the source State. Thus, if interest arising in a Contracting State is received by a nominee or agent that is a resident of the other State on behalf of a person that is not a resident of that other State, the interest is not entitled to the benefits of Article 11. However, interest received by a nominee on behalf of a resident of that other State would be entitled to benefits. These limitations are confirmed by paragraph 9 of the OECD Commentary to Article 11.

Paragraph 3 of Article 11

Paragraph 3 provides for exclusive residence-based taxation in certain cases.

Under subparagraph 3(a), interest beneficially owned by a Contracting State or an instrumentality of that Contracting State which is not subject to tax on its income by that State, (*i.e.*, in the United States, a State or local government) is subject to exclusive residence-based taxation.

Under subparagraph 3(b), interest beneficially owned by a resident of a Contracting State with respect to debt obligations guaranteed or insured by the Contracting State or an instrumentality of that State which is not subject to tax on its income by that State is subject to exclusive residence-based taxation.

Under subparagraph 3(c), interest beneficially owned by a resident of the other Contracting State that is a bank that is unrelated to the payer of the interest or an enterprise substantially deriving its gross income inform the active and regular conduct of a lending of finance business involving transactions with unrelated parties that is unrelated to the payer of the interest is subject to exclusive residence-based taxation.

For purposes of subparagraph 3(c), the term "lending or finance business" is defined to include the business of making loans; purchasing or discounting accounts receivable, notes, or installment obligations; engaging in finance leasing (including entering into finance leases and purchasing, servicing, and disposing of finance leases and related leased assets); issuing letters of credit or providing guarantees; or providing charge and credit card services.

Paragraph 4 of Article 11

Paragraph 4 is in all material respects the same as paragraph 4 of Article 11 of the existing Convention. The only change is the deletion of references to "fixed base" and "Article 14 (Independent Personal Services), to conform to changes made by Article X of the Protocol.

Paragraph 4 provides an exception to the rules of paragraphs 2 and 3 in cases where the beneficial owner of the interest carries on business through a permanent establishment in the State of source and the interest is attributable to that permanent establishment. In such cases the provisions of Article 7 (Business Profits) will apply and the State of source will retain the right to impose tax on such interest income.

In the case of a permanent establishment that once existed in the State but that no longer exists, the provisions of paragraph 4 also apply to interest that would be attributable to such a permanent establishment if it did exist in the year of payment or accrual. See the Technical Explanation to Article V of the Protocol.

Paragraph 5 of Article 11

Paragraph 5 provides a source rule for determining the source of interest that is identical in substance to the interest source rule of the OECD Model. Interest is considered to arise in a Contracting State if paid by that State itself, a political subdivision, a local authority, or a resident of that State. As an exception, interest on a debt incurred in connection with a permanent establishment in one of the States and borne by the permanent establishment is considered to arise in that State. For this purpose, interest is considered to be borne by a permanent establishment if it is allocable to taxable income of that permanent establishment.

Paragraph 6 of Article 11

Paragraph 6 is in all material respects the same as paragraph 6 of Article 11 of the existing Convention. Paragraph 6 provides that in cases involving special relationships between the payor and the beneficial owner of interest income, Article 11 applies only to that portion of the total interest payments that would have been made absent such special relationships (*i.e.*, an arm's-length interest payment). Any excess amount of interest paid remains taxable according to the laws of the United States and New Zealand, respectively, with due regard to the other provisions of the Convention. Thus, if the excess amount would be treated under the source country's law as a distribution of profits by a corporation, such amount could be taxed as a dividend rather than as interest, but the tax would be subject, if appropriate, to the rate limitations of paragraph 2 and 3 of Article 10 (Dividends).

The term "special relationship" is not defined in the Convention. In applying this paragraph the United States considers the term to include the relationships described in Article 9, which in turn corresponds to the definition of "control" for purposes of Code section 482.

This paragraph does not address cases where, owing to a special relationship between the payor and the beneficial owner or between both of them and some other person, the amount of the interest is less than an arm's-length amount. In those cases a transaction may be characterized to reflect its substance and interest may be imputed consistent with the definition of interest in paragraph 7. The United States would apply Code section 482 or 7872 to determine the amount of imputed interest in those cases.

Paragraph 7 of Article 11

The term "interest" as used in Article 11 is defined in paragraph 7 to include, *inter alia*, income from debt claims of every kind, whether or not secured by a mortgage. Penalty charges for late payment are excluded from the definition of interest. Interest that is paid or accrued subject to a contingency is within the ambit of Article 11. This includes income from a debt obligation carrying the right to participate in profits. The term does not, however, include amounts that are treated as dividends under Article 10.

The term interest also includes amounts subject to the same tax treatment as income from money lent under the law of the State in which the income arises. Thus, for purposes of the Convention, amounts that the United States will treat as interest include (i) the difference between the issue price and the stated redemption price at maturity of a debt instrument (*i.e.*, original issue discount ("OID")), which may be wholly or partially realized on the disposition of a debt instrument (section 1273), (ii) amounts that are imputed interest on a deferred sales contract (section 483), (iii) amounts treated as interest or OID under the stripped bond rules (section 1286), (iv) amounts treated as original issue discount under the below-market interest rate rules (section 7872), (v) a partner's distributive share of a partnership's interest income (section 702), (vi) the interest portion of periodic payments made under a "finance lease" or similar contractual arrangement that in substance is a borrowing by the nominal lessee to finance the acquisition of property, (vii) amounts included in the income of a holder of a residual interest in a REMIC (section 860E), because these amounts generally are subject to the same taxation treatment as interest under U.S. tax law, and (viii) interest with respect to notional principal contracts that are re-characterized as loans because of a "substantial non-periodic payment."

Paragraph 8 of Article 11

Paragraph 8 provides anti-abuse exceptions to the rules of paragraphs 1, 2, and 3 for two classes of interest payments.

The first class of interest, dealt with in subparagraph (a) is so-called "contingent interest." With respect to interest arising in the United States, subparagraph (a) refers to contingent interest of a type that does not qualify as portfolio interest under U.S. domestic law. The cross-reference to the U.S. definition of contingent interest, which is found in Code section 871(h)(4), is intended to ensure that the exceptions of Code section 871(h)(4)(c) will be applicable. Any interest dealt with in subparagraph (a) may be taxed in the source State at a rate not exceeding 10 percent of the gross amount of the interest.

The second class of interest is dealt with in subparagraph (b). This exception is consistent with the policy of Code sections 860E(e) and 860G(b) that excess inclusions with respect to a real estate mortgage investment conduit (REMIC) should bear full U.S. tax in all cases. Without a full tax at source foreign purchasers of residual interests would have a competitive advantage over U.S. purchasers at the time these interests are initially offered. Also, absent this rule, the U.S. fisc would suffer a revenue loss with respect to mortgages held in a REMIC because of opportunities for tax avoidance created by differences in the timing of taxable and economic income produced by these interests.

Paragraph 9 of Article 11

Paragraph 9 permits a Contracting State to impose its branch level interest tax on a corporation resident in the other Contracting State. The base of this tax is the excess, if any, of the interest deductible in the first-mentioned Contracting State in computing the profits of the corporation that are subject to tax in the first-mentioned Contracting State and either attributable to a permanent establishment in the first-mentioned Contracting State or subject to tax in the first-mentioned Contracting State under Article 6 (Income from Real Property) or Article 13 (Alienation of Property) of the Convention over the interest paid by the permanent establishment or trade or business in the first-mentioned Contracting State. Such excess interest may be taxed as if it were interest arising in the first- mentioned Contracting State and beneficially owned by the corporation resident in the other Contracting State. Thus, such excess interest may be taxed by the Contracting State of source at a rate not to exceed the 10 percent rate provided for in paragraph 2, and shall be exempt from tax by the Contracting State of source if the recipient is described in paragraph 3.

Paragraph 10 of Article 11

Paragraph 10 provides an exception to the rule of subparagraph 3(c) of this Article. Interest that is beneficially owned by a bank that is unrelated to the payer of the interest or an enterprise substantially deriving its gross income from the active and regular conduct of a lending or finance business involving transactions with unrelated parties that is unrelated to the payer of the interest may be taxed in the State of source at a rate not exceeding 10 percent of the gross amount of the interest if the requirements of either subparagraph 10(a) or (b) are met.

Subparagraph 10(a) was included at the request of New Zealand in order to clarify the coordination of this Article with New Zealand's domestic law. New Zealand's Approved Issuer Levy ("AIL") regime is an alternative to the non-resident withholding tax (the "NRWT") regime. The AIL regime requires New Zealand borrowers who borrow from non-resident unrelated lenders to pay AIL in respect of the interest. The AIL is capped at two percent of the gross amount of the interest, and imposed on the New Zealand borrower, rather than the non-resident lender. The AIL mechanism requires two approvals: 1) the financial arrangement must be a registered security, and 2) the payer of the interest must be an approved issuer. Under New Zealand's domestic law, if the New Zealand borrower pays the AIL, the interest with respect to which the AIL was paid will be exempt from NRWT.

Subparagraph 10(a) allows source country taxation on interest payments at a rate not exceeding 10 percent of the gross amount of the interest if the interest is paid by a person that has not paid the AIL in respect of the interest payment. However, subparagraph 10(a) shall not apply if New Zealand repeals the AIL regime, or the payer of the interest is not eligible to elect to pay the AIL, or if the rate of the AIL payable in respect of such interest exceeds two percent of the gross amount of the interest. The term "approved issuer levy" is intended to include any identical or substantially similar charge payable by the payer of interest arising in New Zealand enacted after the date of this Convention in place of the AIL. Thus, the combined effect of subparagraph 3(c) and paragraph 10 is to preserve the interest withholding exemptions currently provided under New Zealand domestic law.

Subparagraph 10(b) allows source country taxation on interest payments at a rate not exceeding 10 percent of the gross amount of the interest if the interest is paid as a part of a back-to-back loan or an arrangement that is economically similar to and has the effect of a back-to-back loan. By referencing arrangements that are economically similar to, and that have the effect of, a back-to-back loan, subparagraph (10)(b) applies to transactions that would not meet the legal requirements of a loan, but would nevertheless serve that purpose economically. For example, the term would encompass securities issued at a discount, or certain swap arrangements intended to operate as the economic equivalent of a back-to-back loan.

Paragraph 11 of Article 11

Paragraph 11 provides that nothing in Article 11 is intended to limit or restrict, in any manner, the right and ability of a Contracting State to apply and enforce any anti-avoidance provisions of its taxation laws.

Relationship to Other Articles

Notwithstanding the foregoing limitations on source country taxation of interest, the saving clause of paragraph 3 of Article 1 (General Scope) permits the United States to tax its residents and citizens, subject to the special foreign tax credit rules of paragraph 4 of Article 22 (Relief from Double Taxation), as if the Convention had not come into force.

As with other benefits of the Convention, the benefits of this Article are available to a resident of the other State only if that resident is entitled to those benefits under the provisions of Article 16 (Limitation on Benefits).

ARTICLE VIII

Article 8 of the Protocol replaces Article 12 (Royalties) of the Convention, and provides rules for the taxation of royalties arising in one Contracting State and paid to a resident of the other Contracting State.

Paragraph 1 of Article 12

Paragraph 1 is in all material respects the same as paragraph 1 of Article 12 of the existing Convention. Paragraph 1 grants the State of residence the non-exclusive right to tax a royalty arising in the other Contracting State and paid to its residents.

Paragraph 2 of Article 12

Paragraph 2 allows the State of source to tax royalties arising in that State. If, however, the beneficial owner of the royalty is a resident of the other Contracting State, the tax may not exceed 5 percent of the gross amount of the royalties.

The term "beneficial owner" is not defined in the Convention, and is, therefore, defined under the internal law of the State granting treaty benefits (*i.e.*, the State of source). The beneficial owner of the royalty for purposes of Article 12 is the person to which the income is attributable under the laws of the source State. Thus, if a royalty arising in a Contracting State is received by a nominee or agent that is a resident of the other State on behalf of a person that is not a resident of that other State, the royalty is not entitled to the benefits of Article 12. However, a royalty received by a nominee on behalf of a resident of that other State would be entitled to benefits. These limitations are confirmed by paragraph 4 of the OECD Commentary to Article 12.

Paragraph 3 of Article 12

Paragraph 3 defines the term "royalties," as used in this Article, to mean any consideration for the use of, or the right to use, any copyright of literary, artistic, scientific or other work (including cinematographic films and films or video tapes for use in connection with television or tapes for use in connection with radio broadcasting), any patent, trademark, design or model, plan, secret formula or process, or for information concerning industrial, commercial, or scientific experience. The term "royalties" also includes gain derived from the alienation of any right or property that would give rise to royalties, to the extent the gain is contingent on the productivity, use, or further alienation thereof. Gains that are not so contingent are dealt with under Article 13 (Alienation of Property). The Protocol amends the definition of "royalty" by omitting from that definition payments of any kind received as consideration for the use of, or the right to use, industrial, commercial, or scientific equipment other than payments under a hire-purchase agreement.

The term "royalties" is defined in the Convention and therefore is generally independent of domestic law. Certain terms used in the definition are not defined in the Convention, but these may be defined under domestic tax law. For example, the term "secret process or formulas" is found in the Code, and its meaning has been elaborated in the context of Code sections 351 and 367. See Rev. Rul. 55- 17, 1955-1 C.B. 388; Rev. Rul. 64-56, 1964-1 C.B. 133; Rev. Proc. 69- 19, 1969-2 C.B. 301.

Consideration for the use or right to use cinematographic films and films or video tapes for use in connection with television or tapes for use in connection with radio broadcasting is specifically included in the definition of royalties. It is intended that, with respect to any subsequent technological advances in the field of radio or television broadcasting, consideration received for the use of such technology will also be included in the definition of royalties.

If an artist who is resident in one Contracting State records a performance in the other Contracting State, retains a copyrighted interest in a recording, and receives payments for the right to use the recording based on the sale or public playing of the recording, then the right of such other Contracting State to tax those payments is governed by Article 12 of the Convention. See Boulez v. Commissioner, 83 T.C. 584 (1984), aff'd, 810 F.2d 209 (D.C. Cir. 1986). By contrast, if the artist earns in the other Contracting State income covered by Article 17 of the Convention (Artistes and Athletes), for example, endorsement income from the artist's attendance at a film screening, and if such income also is attributable to one of the rights described in Article 12 (*e.g.*, the use of the artist's photograph in promoting the screening), Article 17 and not Article 12 is applicable to such income.

Computer software generally is protected by copyright laws around the world. Under the Convention, consideration received for the use, or the right to use, computer software is treated either as royalties or as business profits, depending on the facts and circumstances of the transaction giving rise to the payment.

The primary factor in determining whether consideration received for the use, or the right to use, computer software is treated as royalties or as business profits is the nature of the rights transferred. See Treas. Reg. section 1.861-18. The fact that the transaction is characterized as a license for copyright law purposes is not dispositive. For example, a typical retail sale of "shrink wrap" software generally will not be considered to give rise to royalty income, even though for copyright law purposes it may be characterized as a license.

The means by which the computer software is transferred are not relevant for purposes of the analysis. Consequently, if software is electronically transferred but the rights obtained by the transferee are substantially equivalent to rights in a program copy, the payment will be considered business profits.

The term "industrial, commercial, or scientific experience" (sometimes referred to as "know-how") has the meaning ascribed to it in paragraph 11 *et seq.* of the Commentary to Article 12 of the OECD Model. Consistent with that meaning, the term may include information that is ancillary to a right otherwise giving rise to royalties, such as a patent or secret process.

Know-how also may include, in limited cases, technical information that is conveyed through technical or consultancy services. It does not include general educational training of the user's employees, nor does it include information developed especially for the user, such as a technical plan or design developed according to the user's specifications. Thus, as provided in paragraph 11.4 of the Commentary to Article 12 of the OECD Model, the term "royalties" does not include payments received as consideration for after-sales service, for services rendered by a seller to a purchaser under a warranty, or for pure technical assistance.

The term "royalties" also does not include payments for professional services (such as architectural, engineering, legal, managerial, medical, software development services). For example, income from the design of a refinery by an engineer (even if the engineer employed know-how in the process of rendering the design) or the production of a legal brief by a lawyer is not income from the transfer of know-how taxable under Article 12, but is income from services taxable under either Article 7 (Business Profits) of the Convention or Article 15 (Dependent Personal Services). Professional services may be embodied in property that gives rise to royalties, however. Thus, if a professional contracts to develop patentable property and retains rights in the resulting property under the development contract, subsequent license payments made for those rights would be royalties.

Paragraph 4 of Article 12

Paragraph 4 is in all material respects the same as paragraph 4 of Article 12 of the existing Convention. The only change is the deletion of references to "fixed base" and "Article 14 (Independent Personal Services), to conform with changes made by Article X of the Protocol. This paragraph provides an exception to the manner of allocating taxing rights specified in paragraph 2 in cases where the beneficial owner of the royalties carries on business through a permanent establishment in the State of source and the royalties are attributable to that permanent establishment. In such cases the provisions of Article 7 (Business Profits) will apply.

The provisions of paragraph 8 of Article 7 apply to this paragraph. For example, royalty income that is attributable to a permanent establishment and that accrues during the existence of the permanent establishment, but is received after the permanent establishment no longer exists, remains taxable under the provisions of Article 7, and not under this Article.

Paragraph 5 of Article 12

Paragraph 5 is in all material respects the same as paragraph 5 of Article 12 of the existing Convention. The only change is the deletion of references to "fixed base." Paragraph 5 contains a source rule for determining the source of royalties. Under paragraph 5, royalties are treated as arising in a Contracting State if paid by a resident of that State. As an exception, royalties that are attributable to a permanent establishment in a Contracting State and borne by the permanent establishment are considered to arise in that State. Where, however, the payor of the royalties is not a resident of either Contracting State, and the royalties are not borne by a permanent establishment in either Contracting State, but the royalties relate to the use of, or the right to use, in one of the Contracting States, any property or right described in paragraph 3, the royalties are deemed to arise in that State.

Paragraph 6 of Article 12

Paragraph 6 is identical to paragraph 6 of Article 12 of the existing Convention. Paragraph 6 provides that in cases involving special relationships between the payor and beneficial owner of royalties, Article 12 applies only to the extent the royalties would have been paid absent such special relationships (*i.e.*, an arm's-length royalty). Any excess amount of royalties paid remains taxable according to the laws of the two Contracting States, with due

Paragraph 3

Paragraph 3 of the Protocol amends Article 13 (Alienation of Property) of the existing Convention by renumbering paragraph 7 as new paragraph 8.

ARTICLE X

To conform to the current U.S. and OECD Model Conventions, Article X of the Protocol deletes Article 14 (Independent Personal Services) of the existing Convention. The subsequent articles of the Convention are not renumbered. Under the provisions of Article 14 prior to its deletion by the Protocol, income from independent personal services could be taxed by the State in which the services were performed if the individual providing the services was present in that State for a period or periods aggregating more than 183 days in any consecutive twelve month period. The effect of the deletion of Article 14 is that income from independent personal services will be governed by the provisions of Articles 5 (Permanent Establishment) and 7 (Business Profits).

Article X of the Protocol also makes corresponding adjustments to remove references to Article 14 and the term "fixed base" from paragraph 4 of Article 6 (Income from Real Property), paragraph 2(c) of Article 15 (Dependent Personal Services), paragraphs 1 and 2 of Article 17 (Artistes and Athletes), and paragraph 3 of Article 19 (Government Service).

ARTICLE XI

Article XI of the Protocol replaces Article 16 (Limitation on Benefits) of the existing Convention. Article 16 contains anti-treaty-shopping provisions that are intended to prevent residents of third countries from benefiting from what is intended to be a reciprocal agreement between two countries. In general, the provision does not rely on a determination of purpose or intention but instead sets forth a series of objective tests. A resident of a Contracting State that satisfies one of the tests will receive benefits regardless of its motivations in choosing its particular business structure.

The structure of the Article is as follows: Paragraph 1 states the general rule that residents are entitled to benefits otherwise accorded to residents only to the extent provided in the Article. Paragraph 2 lists a series of attributes of a resident of a Contracting State, the presence of any one of which will entitle that person to all the benefits of the Convention. Paragraph 3 provides that, regardless of whether a person qualifies for benefits under paragraph 2, benefits may be granted to that person with regard to certain income earned in the conduct of an active trade or business. Paragraph 4 provides that benefits also may be granted if the competent authority of the State from which benefits are claimed determines that it is appropriate to provide benefits in that case. Paragraph 5 provides special rules for so-called "triangular cases" notwithstanding paragraphs 1 through 4 of the Article. Paragraph 6 defines certain terms used in the Article.

Paragraph 1 of Article 16

Paragraph 1 provides that a resident of a Contracting State will be entitled to the benefits otherwise accorded to residents of a Contracting State under the Convention only to the extent provided in the Article. The benefits otherwise accorded to residents under the Convention include all limitations on source-based taxation under Articles 6 (Income from Real Property) through 15 (Dependent Personal Services) and 17 (Artistes and Athletes) through 21 (Other Income), the treaty-based relief from double taxation provided by Article 22 (Relief from Double Taxation), and the protection against discrimination afforded to residents of a Contracting State under Article 23 (Non-Discrimination). Some provisions do not require that a person be a resident in order to enjoy the benefits of those provisions. Article 24 (Mutual Agreement Procedure) is not limited to residents of the Contracting States, and Article 26 (Diplomatic Agents and Consular Officers) applies to diplomatic agents or consular officials regardless of residence. Article 16 accordingly does not limit the availability of treaty benefits under these provisions.

Article 16 and the anti-abuse provisions of domestic law complement each other, as Article 16 effectively determines whether an entity has a sufficient nexus to the Contracting State to be treated as a resident for treaty purposes, while domestic anti-abuse provisions (*e.g.*, business purpose, substance-over-form, step transaction or conduit principles) determine whether a particular transaction should be recast in accordance with its substance. Thus, internal law principles of the source Contracting State may be applied to identify the beneficial owner of an item of income, and Article 16 then will be applied to the beneficial owner to determine if that person is entitled to the benefits of the Convention with respect to such income.

Paragraph 2 of Article 16

Paragraph 2 has five subparagraphs, each of which describes a category of residents that are entitled to all benefits of the Convention.

It is intended that the provisions of paragraph 2 will be self executing. Unlike the provisions of paragraph 4, discussed below, claiming benefits under paragraph 2 does not require an advance competent authority ruling or approval. The tax authorities may, of course, on review, determine that the taxpayer has improperly interpreted the paragraph and is not entitled to the benefits claimed.

Individuals -- Subparagraph 2(a)

Subparagraph (a) provides that individual residents of a Contracting State will be entitled to all treaty benefits. If such an individual receives income as a nominee on behalf of a third country resident, benefits may be denied under the respective articles of the Convention by the requirement that the beneficial owner of the income be a resident of a Contracting State.

Governments -- Subparagraph 2(b)

Subparagraph (b) provides that the Contracting States and any political subdivision or local authority thereof will be entitled to all benefits of the Convention.

Publicly-Traded Corporations -- Subparagraph 2(c)(i)

Subparagraph (c) applies to two categories of companies: publicly traded companies and subsidiaries of publicly traded companies. A company resident in a Contracting State is entitled to all the benefits of the Convention under clause (i) of subparagraph (c) if the principal class of its shares, and any disproportionate class of shares, is regularly traded on one or more recognized stock exchanges and the company satisfies at least one of the following additional requirements: first, the company's principal class of shares is primarily traded on one or more recognized stock exchanges located in the Contracting State of which the company is a resident; or, second, the company's primary place of management and control is in its State of residence.

The term "recognized stock exchange" is defined in subparagraph 6(a). It includes (i) the NASDAQ System and any stock exchange registered with the Securities and Exchange Commission as a national securities exchange for purposes of the Securities Exchange Act of 1934; (ii) the New Zealand Stock Market; and (iii) any other stock exchange agreed upon by the competent authorities of the Contracting States.

If a company has only one class of shares, it is only necessary to consider whether the shares of that class meet the relevant trading requirements. If the company has more than one class of shares, it is necessary as an initial matter to determine which class or classes constitute the "principal class of shares". The term "principal class of shares" is defined in subparagraph 6(b) to mean the ordinary or common shares of the company representing the majority of the aggregate voting power and value of the company. If the company does not have a class of ordinary or common shares representing the majority of the aggregate voting power and value of the company, then the "principal class of shares" is that class or any combination of classes of shares that represents, in the aggregate, a majority of the voting power and value of the company. Although in a particular case involving a company with several classes of shares it is conceivable that more than one group of classes could be identified that account for more than 50% of the shares, it is only necessary for one such group to satisfy the requirements of this subparagraph in order for the company to be entitled to benefits. Benefits would not be denied to the company even if a second, non-qualifying, group of shares with more than half of the company's voting power and value could be identified.

A company whose principal class of shares is regularly traded on a recognized stock exchange will nevertheless not qualify for benefits under subparagraph 2(c) if it has a disproportionate class of shares that is not regularly traded on a recognized stock exchange. The term "disproportionate class of shares" is defined in subparagraph 6(c). A company has a disproportionate class of shares if it has outstanding a class of shares that is subject to terms or other arrangements that entitle the holder to a larger portion of the company's income, profit, or gain in the other Contracting State than that to which the holder would be entitled in the absence of such terms or arrangements. Thus, for example, a company resident in New Zealand has a disproportionate class of shares if it has outstanding a class of "tracking stock" that pays dividends based upon a formula that approximates the company's return on its assets employed in the United States.

The following example illustrates this result.

Example. NZCo is a corporation resident in New Zealand. NZCo has two classes of shares: Common and Preferred. The Common shares are listed and regularly traded on the New Zealand Stock Market. The Preferred shares have no voting rights and are entitled to receive dividends equal in amount to interest payments that NZCo receives from unrelated borrowers in the United States. The Preferred shares are owned entirely by a single investor that is a resident of a country with which the United States does not have a tax treaty. The Common shares account for more than 50 percent of the value of NZCo and for 100 percent of the voting power. Because the owner of the Preferred shares is entitled to receive payments corresponding to the U.S. source interest income earned by NZCo, the Preferred shares are a disproportionate class of shares. Because the Preferred shares are not regularly traded on a recognized stock exchange, NZCo will not qualify for benefits under subparagraph 2(c).

The term "regularly traded" is not defined in the Convention. In accordance with paragraph 2 of Article 3 (General Definitions), this term will be defined by reference to the domestic tax laws of the State from which treaty benefits are sought, generally the source State. In the case of the United States, this term is understood to have the meaning it has under Treas. Reg. section 1.884-5(d)(4)(i)(B), relating to the branch tax provisions of the Code. Under these regulations, a class of shares is considered to be "regularly traded" if two requirements are met: trades in the class of shares are made in more than de minimis quantities on at least 60 days during the taxable year, and the aggregate number of shares in the class traded during the year is at least 10 percent of the average number of shares outstanding during the year. Sections 1.884-5(d)(4)(i)(A), (ii) and (iii) will not be taken into account for purposes of defining the term "regularly traded" under the Convention.

The regular trading requirement can be met by trading on any recognized exchange or exchanges located in either State. Trading on one or more recognized stock exchanges may be aggregated for purposes of this requirement. Thus, a U.S. company could satisfy the regularly traded requirement through trading, in whole or in part, on a recognized stock exchange located in New Zealand. Authorized but unissued shares are not considered for purposes of this test.

The term "primarily traded" is not defined in the Convention. In accordance with paragraph 2 of Article 3 (General Definitions) , this term will have the meaning it has under the laws of the State concerning the taxes to which the Convention applies, generally the source State. In the case of the United States, this term is understood to have the meaning it has under Treas. Reg. section 1.884-5(d)(3), relating to the branch tax provisions of the Code. Accordingly, stock of a corporation is "primarily traded" if the number of shares in the company's principal class of shares that are traded during the taxable year on all recognized stock exchanges in the Contracting State of which the company is a resident exceeds the number of shares in the company's principal class of shares that are traded during that year on established securities markets in any other single foreign country.

A company whose principal class of shares is regularly traded on a recognized exchange but cannot meet the primarily traded test may claim treaty benefits if its primary place of management and control is in its country of residence. This test should be distinguished from the "place of effective management" test which is used in the OECD Model and by many other countries to establish residence. In some cases, the place of effective management test has been interpreted to mean the place where the board of directors meets. By contrast, the primary place of management and control test looks to where day-to-day responsibility for the management of the company (and its subsidiaries) is exercised. The company's primary place of management and control will be located in the State in which the company is a resident only if the executive officers and senior management employees exercise day-to-day responsibility for more of the strategic, financial and operational policy decision making for the company (including direct and indirect subsidiaries) in that State than in the other State or any third state, and the staff that support the management in making those decisions are also based in that State. Thus, the test looks to the overall activities of the relevant persons to see where those activities are conducted. In most cases, it will be a necessary, but not a sufficient, condition that the headquarters of the company (that is, the place at which the Chief Executive Officer and other top executives normally are based) be located in the Contracting State of which the company is a resident.

To apply the test, it will be necessary to determine which persons are to be considered "executive officers and senior management employees". In most cases, it will not be necessary to look beyond the executives who are members of the board of directors (the "inside directors") in the case of a U.S. company. That will not always be the case, however; in fact, the relevant persons may be employees of subsidiaries if those persons make the strategic, financial and operational policy decisions. Moreover, it would be necessary to take into account any special voting arrangements that result in certain board members making certain decisions without the participation of other board members.

Subsidiaries of Publicly-Traded Corporations -- Subparagraph 2(c)(ii)

A company resident in a Contracting State is entitled to all the benefits of the Convention under clause (ii) of subparagraph 2(c) if five or fewer publicly traded companies described in clause (i) are the direct or indirect owners of at least 50 percent of the aggregate vote and value of the company's shares (and at least 50 percent of any disproportionate class of shares). If the publicly-traded companies are indirect owners, however, each of the intermediate companies must be a resident of one of the Contracting States.

Thus, for example, a company that is a resident of New Zealand, all the shares of which are owned by another company that is a resident of New Zealand, would qualify for benefits under the Convention if the principal class of shares (and any disproportionate classes of shares) of the parent company are regularly and primarily traded on a recognized stock exchange in New Zealand. However, such a subsidiary would not qualify for benefits under clause (ii) if the publicly traded parent company were a resident of a third state, for example, and not a resident of the United States or New Zealand. Furthermore, if a parent company in New Zealand indirectly owned the bottom-tier company through a chain of subsidiaries, each

35

such subsidiary in the chain, as an intermediate owner, must be a resident of the United States or New Zealand in order for the subsidiary to meet the test in clause (ii).

Tax Exempt Organizations -- Subparagraph 2(d)

Subparagraph 2(d) provides rules by which the tax exempt organizations described in subparagraphs 1(a) and (b) of Article 4 (Resident) will be entitled to all the benefits of the Convention. A pension fund, as defined in subparagraph 1(l) of Article 3 (General Definitions), will qualify for benefits if more than fifty percent of the beneficiaries, members or participants of the organization are individuals resident in either Contracting State. For purposes of this provision, the term "beneficiaries" should be understood to refer to the persons receiving benefits from the organization. On the other hand, a tax-exempt organization other than a pension fund automatically qualifies for benefits, without regard to the residence of its beneficiaries or members. Entities qualifying under this rule are those that are generally exempt from tax in their State of residence and that are organized and operated exclusively to fulfill religious, charitable, scientific, artistic, cultural, or educational purposes.

Ownership/Base Erosion -- Subparagraph 2(e)

Subparagraph 2(e) provides an additional method to qualify for treaty benefits that applies to any form of legal entity that is a resident of a Contracting State. The test provided in subparagraph (e), the so-called ownership and base erosion test, is a two-part test. Both prongs of the test must be satisfied for the resident to be entitled to treaty benefits under subparagraph 2(e).

The ownership prong of the test, under clause (i), requires that at least 50 percent of the aggregate voting power and value (and at least 50 percent of any disproportionate class of shares) of shares or other beneficial interests in the person is owned, directly or indirectly, on at least half the days of the person's taxable year by persons who are residents of the Contracting State of which that person is a resident and that are themselves entitled to treaty benefits under subparagraphs 2(a), (b), (c)(i), or (d). In the case of indirect owners, each of the intermediate owners must be a resident of that Contracting State.

Trusts may be entitled to benefits under this provision if they are treated as residents under Article 4 (Resident) and they otherwise satisfy the requirements of this subparagraph. For purposes of this subparagraph, the beneficial interests in a trust will be considered to be owned by its beneficiaries in proportion to each beneficiary's actuarial interest in the trust. The interest of a remainder beneficiary will be equal to 100 percent less the aggregate percentages held by income beneficiaries. A beneficiary's interest in a trust will not be considered to be owned by a person entitled to benefits under the other provisions of paragraph 2 if it is not possible to determine the beneficiary's actuarial interest. Consequently, if it is not possible to determine the actuarial interest of the beneficiaries in a trust, the ownership test under clause i) cannot be satisfied, unless all possible beneficiaries are persons entitled to benefits under subparagraphs 2(a), (b), (c)(i), or (d).

The base erosion prong of clause (ii) of subparagraph (e) is satisfied with respect to a person if less than 50 percent of the person's gross income for the taxable year, as determined under the tax law in the person's State of residence, is paid or accrued, directly or indirectly, to persons who are not residents of either Contracting State entitled to benefits under subparagraphs (a), (b), (c)(i), or (d), in the form of payments deductible for tax purposes in the payor's State of residence. These amounts do not include arm's-length payments in the ordinary course of business for services or tangible property, or payments in respect of financial obligations to a bank, provided that such bank is not related to the payor. To the extent they are deductible from the taxable base, trust distributions are deductible payments. However, depreciation and amortization deductions, which do not represent payments or accruals to other persons, are disregarded for this purpose.

Paragraph 3 of Article 16

Paragraph 3 sets forth an alternative test under which a resident of a Contracting State may receive treaty benefits with respect to certain items of income that are connected to an active trade or business conducted in its State of residence. A resident of a Contracting State may qualify for benefits under paragraph 3 whether or not it also qualifies under paragraph 2.

Subparagraph 3(a) sets forth the general rule that a resident of a Contracting State engaged in the active conduct of a trade or business in that State may obtain the benefits of the Convention with respect to an item of income derived in the other Contracting State. The item of income, however, must be derived in connection with or incidental to that trade or business.

The term "trade or business" is not defined in the Convention. Pursuant to paragraph 3 of Article 3, when determining whether a resident of New Zealand is entitled to the benefits of the Convention under paragraph 3 of this Article with respect to an item of income derived from sources within the United States, the United States will ascribe to this term the meaning that it has under the law of the United States. Accordingly, the U.S. competent authority will refer to the regulations issued under Code section 367(a) for the definition of the term "trade or business." In general, therefore, a trade or business will be considered to be a specific unified group of activities that constitute or could constitute an independent economic enterprise carried on for profit. Furthermore, a corporation generally will be considered to carry on a trade or business only if the officers and employees of the corporation conduct substantial managerial and operational activities.

The business of making or managing investments for the resident's own account will be considered to be a trade or business only when part of banking, insurance or securities activities conducted by a bank, an insurance company, or a registered securities dealer. Such activities conducted by a person other than a bank, insurance company or registered securities dealer will not be considered to be the conduct of an active trade or business, nor would they be considered to be the conduct of an active trade or business if conducted by a bank, insurance company or registered securities dealer but not as part of the company's banking, insurance or dealer business. Because a headquarters operation is in the business of managing investments, a company that functions solely as a headquarters company will not be considered to be engaged in an active trade or business for purposes of paragraph 3.

An item of income is derived in connection with a trade or business if the income-producing activity in the State of source is a line of business that "forms a part of" or is "complementary" to the trade or business conducted in the State of residence by the income recipient.

A business activity generally will be considered to form part of a business activity conducted in the State of source if the two activities involve the design, manufacture or sale of the same products or type of products, or the provision of similar services. The line of business in the State of residence may be upstream, downstream, or parallel to the activity conducted in the State of source. Thus, the line of business may provide inputs for a manufacturing process that occurs in the State of source, may sell the output of that manufacturing process, or simply may sell the same sorts of products that are being sold by the trade or business carried on in the State of source.

Example 1. USCo is a corporation resident in the United States. USCo is engaged in an active manufacturing business in the United States. USCo owns 100 percent of the shares of NZCo, a corporation resident in New Zealand. NZCo distributes USCo products in New Zealand. Since the business activities conducted by the two corporations involve the same products, NZCo's distribution business is considered to form a part of USCo's manufacturing business.

Example 2. The facts are the same as in Example 1, except that USCo does not manufacture. Rather, USCo operates a large research and development facility in the United States that licenses intellectual property to affiliates worldwide, including NZCo. NZCo and other USCo affiliates then manufacture and market the USCo-designed products in their respective markets. Since the activities conducted by NZCo and USCo involve the same product lines, these activities are considered to form a part of the same trade or business.

For two activities to be considered to be "complementary," the activities need not relate to the same types of products or services, but they should be part of the same overall industry and be related in the sense that the success or failure of one activity will tend to result in success or failure for the other. Where more than one trade or business is conducted in the State of source and only one of the trades or businesses forms a part of or is complementary to a trade or business conducted in the State of residence, it is necessary to identify the trade or business to which an item of income is attributable. Royalties generally will be considered to be derived in connection with the trade or business to which the underlying intangible property is attributable. Dividends will be deemed to be derived first out of earnings and profits of the treaty-benefited trade or business, and then out of other earnings and profits. Interest income may be allocated under any reasonable method consistently applied. A method that conforms to U.S. principles for expense allocation will be considered a reasonable method.

Example 3. Americair is a corporation resident in the United States that operates an international airline. NZSub is a wholly-owned subsidiary of Americair resident in New Zealand. NZSub operates a chain of hotels in New Zealand that are located near airports served by Americair flights. Americair frequently sells tour packages that include air travel to New

Zealand and lodging at NZSub hotels. Although both companies are engaged in the active conduct of a trade or business, the businesses of operating a chain of hotels and operating an airline are distinct trades or businesses. Therefore NZSub's business does not form a part of Americair's business. However, NZSub's business is considered to be complementary to Americair's business because they are part of the same overall industry (travel) and the links between their operations tend to make them interdependent.

Example 4. The facts are the same as in Example 3, except that NZSub owns an office building in New Zealand instead of a hotel chain. No part of Americair's business is conducted through the office building. NZSub's business is not considered to form a part of or to be complementary to Americair's business. They are engaged in distinct trades or businesses in separate industries, and there is no economic dependence between the two operations.

Example 5. USFlower is a corporation resident in the United States. USFlower produces and sells flowers in the United States and other countries. USFlower owns all the shares of NZHolding, a corporation resident in New Zealand. NZHolding is a holding company that is not engaged in a trade or business. NZHolding owns all the shares of three corporations that are resident in New Zealand: NZFlower, NZLawn, and NZFish. NZFlower distributes USFlower flowers under the USFlower trademark in New Zealand. NZLawn markets a line of lawn care products in New Zealand under the USFlower trademark. In addition to being sold under the same trademark, NZLawn and NZFlower products are sold in the same stores and sales of each company's products tend to generate increased sales of the other's products. NZFish imports fish from the United States and distributes it to fish wholesalers in New Zealand. For purposes of paragraph 3, the business of NZFlower forms a part of the business of USFlower, the business of NZLawn is complementary to the business of USFlower, and the business of NZFish is neither part of nor complementary to that of USFlower.

An item of income derived from the State of source is "incidental to" the trade or business carried on in the State of residence if production of the item facilitates the conduct of the trade or business in the State of residence. An example of incidental income is the temporary investment of working capital of a person in the State of residence in securities issued by persons in the State of source.

Subparagraph 3(b) states a further condition to the general rule in subparagraph (a) in cases where the trade or business generating the item of income in question is carried on either by the person deriving the income or by any associated enterprises. Subparagraph (b) states that the trade or business carried on in the State of residence, under these circumstances, must be substantial in relation to the activity in the State of source. The substantiality requirement is intended to prevent a narrow case of treaty-shopping abuses in which a company attempts to qualify for benefits by engaging in de minimis connected business activities in the treaty country in which it is resident (*i.e.*, activities that have little economic cost or effect with respect to the company business as a whole).

The determination of substantiality is made based upon all the facts and circumstances and takes into account the comparative sizes of the trades or businesses in each Contracting

State, the nature of the activities performed in each Contracting State, and the relative contributions made to that trade or business in each Contracting State.

The determination in subparagraph 3(b) also is made separately for each item of income derived from the State of source. It therefore is possible that a person would be entitled to the benefits of the Convention with respect to one item of income but not with respect to another. If a resident of a Contracting State is entitled to treaty benefits with respect to a particular item of income under paragraph 3, the resident is entitled to all benefits of the Convention insofar as they affect the taxation of that item of income in the State of source.

The application of the substantiality requirement only to income from related parties focuses only on potential abuse cases, and does not hamper certain other kinds of non-abusive activities, even though the income recipient resident in a Contracting State may be very small in relation to the entity generating income in the other Contracting State. For example, if a small U.S. research firm develops a process that it licenses to a very large, unrelated, pharmaceutical manufacturer in New Zealand, the size of the U.S. research firm would not have to be tested against the size of the manufacturer. Similarly, a small U.S. bank that makes a loan to a very large unrelated company operating a business in New Zealand would not have to pass a substantiality test to receive treaty benefits under paragraph 3.

Subparagraph 3(c) provides special attribution rules for purposes of applying the substantive rules of subparagraphs (a) and (b). These rules apply for purposes of determining whether a person meets the requirement in subparagraph (a) that it be engaged in the active conduct of a trade or business and that the item of income is derived in connection with that active trade or business, and for making the comparison required by the "substantiality" requirement in subparagraph (b). Subparagraph (c) attributes to a person activities conducted by persons "connected" to such person. A person ("X") is connected to another person ("Y") if X possesses 50 percent or more of the beneficial interest in Y (or if Y possesses 50 percent or more of the beneficial interest in X). For this purpose, X is connected to a company if X owns shares representing fifty percent or more of the aggregate voting power and value of the company or fifty percent or more of the beneficial equity interest in the company. X also is connected to Y if a third person possesses, directly or indirectly, fifty percent or more of the beneficial interest in both X and Y. For this purpose, if X or Y is a company, the threshold relationship with respect to such company or companies is fifty percent or more of the aggregate voting power and value or fifty percent or more of the beneficial equity interest. Finally, X is connected to Y if, based upon all the facts and circumstances, X controls Y, Y controls X, or X and Y are controlled by the same person or persons.

Paragraph 4 of Article 16

Paragraph 4 provides that a resident of one of the States that is not entitled to the benefits of the Convention as a result of paragraphs 2 through 3 still may be granted benefits under the Convention at the discretion of the competent authority of the State from which benefits are claimed. Under paragraph 4, that competent authority will determine whether the establishment, acquisition, or maintenance of the person seeking benefits under the Convention, or the conduct of such person's operations, has or had as one of its principal purposes the obtaining of benefits under the Convention. Benefits will not be granted, however, solely because a company was established prior to the effective date of a treaty or protocol. In that case a company would still be required to establish to the satisfaction of the competent authority clear non-tax business reasons for its formation in a Contracting State, or that the allowance of benefits would not otherwise be contrary to the purposes of the treaty. Thus, persons that establish operations in one of the States with a principal purpose of obtaining the benefits of the Convention ordinarily will not be granted relief under paragraph 4.

The competent authority's discretion is quite broad. It may grant all of the benefits of the Convention to the taxpayer making the request, or it may grant only certain benefits. For instance, it may grant benefits only with respect to a particular item of income in a manner similar to paragraph 3. Further, the competent authority may establish conditions, such as setting time limits on the duration of any relief granted.

For purposes of implementing paragraph 4, a taxpayer will be permitted to present his case to the relevant competent authority for an advance determination based on the facts. In these circumstances, it is also expected that, if the competent authority determines that benefits are to be allowed, they will be allowed retroactively to the time of entry into force of the relevant treaty provision or the establishment of the structure in question, whichever is later.

Finally, there may be cases in which a resident of a Contracting State may apply for discretionary relief to the competent authority of his State of residence. This would arise, for example, if the benefit the resident is claiming is provided by the residence country, and not by the source country. So, for example, if a company that is a resident of the United States would like to claim the benefit of the re-sourcing rule of paragraph 4 of Article 22, but it does not meet any of the objective tests of this Article, it may apply to the U.S. competent authority for discretionary relief.

Paragraph 5 of Article 16

Paragraph 5 deals with the treatment of income in the context of a so-called "triangular case."

An example of a triangular case would be a structure under which a resident of New Zealand earns interest income from the United States. The resident of New Zealand, who is assumed to qualify for benefits under one or more of the provisions of Article 16, sets up a permanent establishment in a third jurisdiction that imposes only a low rate of tax on the income of the permanent establishment. The New Zealand resident lends funds into the United States through the permanent establishment. The permanent establishment, despite its third-jurisdiction location, is an integral part of a New Zealand resident. Therefore the income that it earns on those loans, absent the provisions of paragraph 5, is entitled to exemption from U.S. withholding tax under the Convention. Under a current New Zealand income tax treaty with the host jurisdiction of the permanent establishment, the income of the permanent establishment is exempt from New Zealand tax (alternatively, New Zealand may choose to exempt the income of the permanent establishment from New Zealand income tax by statute). Thus, the interest income is exempt from U.S. tax, is subject to little tax in the host jurisdiction of the permanent establishment, and is exempt from New Zealand tax.

Paragraph 5 applies reciprocally. However, the United States does not exempt the profits of a third-jurisdiction permanent establishment of a U.S. resident from U.S. tax, either by statute or by treaty.

Paragraph 5 provides that the tax benefits that would otherwise apply under the Convention will not apply to any item of income if the combined tax actually paid in the residence State and the third state is less than 60 percent of the tax that would have been payable in the residence State if the income were earned in that State by the enterprise and were not attributable to the permanent establishment in the third state. In the case of dividends, interest and royalties to which this paragraph applies, the withholding tax rates under the Convention are replaced with a 15 percent withholding tax. Any other income to which the provisions of paragraph 5 apply is subject to tax under the domestic law of the source State, notwithstanding any other provisions of the Convention.

In general, the principles employed under Code section 954(b)(4) will be employed to determine whether the profits are subject to an effective rate of taxation that is above the specified threshold.

Notwithstanding the level of tax on interest and royalty income of the permanent establishment, paragraph 5 will not apply under certain circumstances. In the case of royalties, paragraph 5 will not apply if the royalties are received as compensation for the use of, or the right to use, intangible property produced or developed by the permanent establishment itself. In the case of any other income, paragraph 5 will not apply if that income is derived in connection with, or is incidental to, the active conduct of a trade or business carried on by the permanent establishment in the third state. The business of making, managing or simply holding investments is not considered to be an active trade or business, unless these are banking or securities activities carried on by a bank or registered securities dealer.

Paragraph 6 of Article 16

Paragraph 6 defines several key terms for purposes of Article 16. Each of the defined terms is discussed above in the context in which it is used.

ARTICLE XII

Paragraph 1

Paragraph 1 of Article XII of the Protocol deletes and replaces the last sentence of paragraph 1 of Article 22 (Relief from Double Taxation) of the existing Convention, so that for purposes of this paragraph, the taxes set out in subparagraph 3(a) and paragraph 4 of Article 2 (Taxes Covered) shall be considered income taxes.

Paragraph 2

Paragraph 2 of Article XII of the Protocol deletes the final sentence from paragraph 2 of Article 22 (Relief from Double Taxation) of the existing Convention to account for changes to New Zealand's domestic law.

Paragraph 3

Paragraph 3 of Article 12 of the Protocol replaces paragraph 5 of Article 22 of the existing Convention to conform with changes to Article 2 (Taxes Covered) made in Article II of the Protocol.

ARTICLE XIII

Article XIII of the Protocol replaces Article 23 (Non-discrimination) of the existing Convention. This Article ensures that nationals of a Contracting State, in the case of paragraph 1, and residents of a Contracting State, in the case of paragraphs 2 through 5, will not be subject, directly or indirectly, to discriminatory taxation in the other Contracting State. Not all differences in tax treatment, either as between nationals of the two States, or between residents of the two States, are violations of the prohibition against discrimination. Rather, the non-discrimination obligations of this Article apply only if the nationals or residents of the two States are comparably situated.

Each of the relevant paragraphs of the Article provides that two persons that are comparably situated must be treated similarly. Although the actual words differ from paragraph to paragraph (*e.g.*, paragraph 1 refers to two nationals "in the same circumstances," paragraph 2 refers to two enterprises "carrying on the same activities" and paragraph 4 refers to two enterprises that are "similar"), the common underlying premise is that if the difference in treatment is directly related to a tax-relevant difference in the situations of the domestic and foreign persons being compared, that difference is not to be treated as discriminatory (*i.e.*, if one person is taxable in a Contracting State on worldwide income and the other is not, or tax may be collectible from one person at a later stage, but not from the other, distinctions in treatment would be justified under paragraph 1). Other examples of such factors that can lead to non-discriminatory differences in treatment are noted in the discussions of each paragraph.

The operative paragraphs of the Article also use different language to identify the kinds of differences in taxation treatment that will be considered discriminatory. For example, paragraphs 1 and 4 speak of "any taxation or any requirement connected therewith that is more burdensome," while paragraph 2 specifies that a tax "shall not be less favorably levied." Regardless of these differences in language, only differences in tax treatment that materially disadvantage the foreign person relative to the domestic person are properly the subject of the Article.

Paragraph 1 of Article 23

Paragraph 1 provides that a national of one Contracting State may not be subject to taxation or connected requirements in the other Contracting State that are more burdensome than the taxes and connected requirements imposed upon a national of that other State in the same circumstances. The OECD Model language would prohibit taxation that is "other than or more burdensome" than that imposed on U.S. persons. This Convention omits the reference to taxation that is "other than" that imposed on U.S. persons because the only relevant question under this provision should be whether the requirement imposed on a national of the other Contracting State is more burdensome. A requirement may be different from the requirements imposed on U.S. nationals without being more burdensome.

The term "national" in relation to a Contracting State is defined in subparagraph 1(k) of Article 3 (General Definitions). The term includes both individuals and juridical persons. A national of a Contracting State is afforded protection under this paragraph even if the national is not a resident of either Contracting State. Thus, a U.S. citizen who is resident in a third country is entitled, under this paragraph, to the same treatment in New Zealand as a national of New Zealand who is in similar circumstances (*i.e.*, presumably one who is resident in a third State).

As noted above, whether or not the two persons are both taxable on worldwide income is a significant circumstance for this purpose. For this reason, paragraph 1 specifically states that the United States is not obligated to apply the same taxing regime to a national of New Zealand who is not resident in the United States as it applies to a U.S. national who is not resident in the United States. United States citizens who are not residents of the United States but who are, nevertheless, subject to United States tax on their worldwide income are not in the same circumstances with respect to United States taxation as citizens of New Zealand who are not United States residents. Thus, for example, Article 23 would not entitle a national of New Zealand resident in a third country to taxation at graduated rates on U.S. source dividends or other investment income that applies to a U.S. citizen resident in the same third country.

Paragraph 2 of Article 23

Paragraph 2 provides that a Contracting State may not tax a permanent establishment of an enterprise of the other Contracting State less favorably than an enterprise of that first-mentioned State that is carrying on the same activities.

The fact that a U.S. permanent establishment of an enterprise of New Zealand is subject to U.S. tax only on income that is attributable to the permanent establishment, while a U.S. corporation engaged in the same activities is taxable on its worldwide income is not, in itself, a sufficient difference to provide different treatment for the permanent establishment. There are cases, however, where the two enterprises would not be similarly situated and differences in treatment may be warranted. For instance, it would not be a violation of the non-discrimination protection of paragraph 2 to require the foreign enterprise to provide information in a reasonable manner that may be different from the information requirements imposed on a resident enterprise, because information may not be as readily available to the Internal Revenue Service from a foreign as from a domestic enterprise. Similarly, it would not be a violation of paragraph 2 to impose penalties on persons who fail to comply with such a requirement (see, *e.g.*, Code sections 874(a) and 882(c)(2)). Further, a determination that income and expenses have been attributed or allocated to a permanent establishment in conformity with the principles of Article 7 (Business Profits) implies that the attribution or allocation was not discriminatory.

Section 1446 of the Code imposes on any partnership with income that is effectively connected with a U.S. trade or business the obligation to withhold tax on amounts allocable to a foreign partner. In the context of the Convention, this obligation applies with respect to a share of the partnership income of a partner resident in New Zealand, and attributable to a U.S. permanent establishment. There is no similar obligation with respect to the distributive shares of U.S. resident partners. It is understood, however, that this distinction is not a form of discrimination within the meaning of paragraph 2 of the Article. No distinction is made between U.S. and non-U.S. partnerships, since the law requires that partnerships of both U.S. and non-U.S. domicile withhold tax in respect of the partnership shares of non-U.S. partners. Furthermore, in distinguishing between U.S. and non-U.S. partners, the requirement to withhold on the non-U.S. but not the U.S. partner's share is not discriminatory taxation, but, like other withholding on nonresident aliens, is merely a reasonable method for the collection of tax from persons who are not continually present in the United States, and as to whom it otherwise may be difficult for the United States to enforce its tax jurisdiction. If tax has been over-withheld, the partner can, as in other cases of over-withholding, file for a refund.

Paragraph 3 of Article 23

Paragraph 3 makes clear that the provisions of paragraphs 1 and 2 do not obligate a Contracting State to grant to a resident of the other Contracting State any tax allowances, reliefs, etc., that it grants to its own residents on account of their civil status or family responsibilities. Thus, if a sole proprietor who is a resident of New Zealand has a permanent establishment in the United States, in assessing income tax on the profits attributable to the permanent establishment, the United States is not obligated to allow to the resident of New Zealand the personal allowances for himself and his family that he would be permitted to take if the permanent establishment were a sole proprietorship owned and operated by a U.S. resident, despite the fact that the individual income tax rates would apply.

Paragraph 4 of Article 23

Paragraph 4 is identical to paragraph 3 of Article 23 of the existing Convention. Paragraph 4 prohibits discrimination in the allowance of deductions. When a resident or an enterprise of a Contracting State pays interest, royalties or other disbursements to a resident of the other Contracting State, the first-mentioned Contracting State must allow a deduction for those payments in computing the taxable profits of the resident or enterprise as if the payment had been made under the same conditions to a resident of the first-mentioned Contracting State. Paragraph 4, however, does not require a Contracting State to give non-residents more favorable treatment than it gives to its own residents. Consequently, a Contracting State does not have to allow non-residents a deduction for items that are not deductible under its domestic law (for example, expenses of a capital nature).

The term "other disbursements" is understood to include a reasonable allocation of executive and general administrative expenses, research and development expenses and other expenses incurred for the benefit of a group of related persons that includes the person incurring the expense.

An exception to the rule of paragraph 4 is provided for cases where the provisions of paragraph 1 of Article 9 (Associated Enterprises), paragraph 6 of Article 11 (Interest) or paragraph 6 of Article 12 (Royalties) apply. All of these provisions permit the denial of deductions in certain circumstances in respect of transactions between related persons. Neither State is forced to apply the non-discrimination principle in such cases. The exception with respect to paragraph 6 of Article 11 would include the denial or deferral of certain interest deductions under Code section 163(j).

Paragraph 5 of Article 23

Paragraph 5 requires that a Contracting State not impose more burdensome taxation or connected requirements on an enterprise of that State that is wholly or partly owned or controlled, directly or indirectly, by one or more residents of the other Contracting State than the taxation or connected requirements that it imposes on other similar enterprises of that first-mentioned Contracting State. For this purpose it is understood that "similar" refers to similar activities or ownership of the enterprise.

This rule, like all non-discrimination provisions, does not prohibit differing treatment of entities that are in differing circumstances. Rather, a protected enterprise is only required to be treated in the same manner as other enterprises that, from the point of view of the application of the tax law, are in substantially similar circumstances both in law and in fact. The taxation of a distributing corporation under Code section 367(e) on an applicable distribution to foreign shareholders does not violate paragraph 5 of the Article because a foreign-owned corporation is not similar to a domestically-owned corporation that is accorded non-recognition treatment under Code sections 337 and 355.

For the reasons given above in connection with the discussion of paragraph 2 of the Article, it is also understood that the provision in Code section 1446 for withholding of tax on non-U.S. partners does not violate paragraph 5 of the Article.

It is further understood that the ineligibility of a U.S. corporation with nonresident alien shareholders to make an election to be an "S" corporation does not violate paragraph 5 of the Article. If a corporation elects to be an S corporation, it is generally not subject to income tax and the shareholders take into account their pro rata shares of the corporation's items of income, loss, deduction or credit. (The purpose of the provision is to allow an individual or small group of individuals the protections of conducting business in corporate form while paying taxes at individual rates as if the business were conducted directly.) A nonresident alien does not pay U.S. tax on a net basis, and, thus, does not generally take into account items of loss, deduction or credit. Thus, the S corporation provisions do not exclude corporations with nonresident alien shareholders because such shareholders are foreign, but only because they are not net-basis taxpayers. Similarly, the provisions exclude corporations with other types of shareholders where the purpose of the provisions cannot be fulfilled or their mechanics implemented. For example, corporations with corporate shareholders are excluded because the purpose of the provision to permit individuals to conduct a business in corporate form at individual tax rates would not be furthered by their inclusion.

Finally, it is understood that paragraph 5 does not require a Contracting State to allow foreign corporations to join in filing a consolidated return with a domestic corporation or to allow similar benefits between domestic and foreign enterprises.

Paragraph 6 of Article 23

Paragraph 6 of the Article confirms that no provision of the Article will prevent either Contracting State from imposing either the branch profits tax described in paragraph 8 of Article 10 (Dividends).

Paragraph 7 of Article 23

Paragraph 7 of the Article states that the Article shall not apply to any provision of the taxation laws of the Contracting State which is reasonably designed to prevent or defeat the avoidance or evasion of taxes.

Relationship to Other Articles

The saving clause of paragraph 3 of Article 1 (General Scope) does not apply to this Article by virtue of the exceptions in paragraph 4(a) of Article 1. Thus, for example, a U.S. citizen who is a resident of New Zealand may claim benefits in the United States under this Article.

Nationals of a Contracting State may claim the benefits of paragraph 1 regardless of whether they are entitled to benefits under Article 16 (Limitation on Benefits), because that paragraph applies to nationals and not residents. They may not claim the benefits of the other paragraphs of this Article with respect to an item of income unless they are generally entitled to treaty benefits with respect to that income under a provision of Article 16.

ARTICLE XIV

Article XIV of the Protocol replaces Article 25 (Exchange of Information and Administrative Assistance) of the existing Convention. This Article provides for the exchange of information and administrative assistance between the competent authorities of the Contracting States.

Paragraph 1 of Article 25

The obligation to obtain and provide information to the other Contracting State is set out in Paragraph 1. The information to be exchanged is that which may be relevant for carrying out the provisions of the Convention or the domestic laws of the United States or of New Zealand concerning taxes of every kind applied at the national level. This language incorporates the standard in 26 U.S.C. Section 7602 which authorizes the IRS to examine "any books, papers, records, or other data which may be relevant or material." (Emphasis added.) In United States v. Arthur Young & Co., 465 U.S. 805, 814 (1984), the Supreme Court stated that the language "may be" reflects Congress's express intention to allow the IRS to obtain "items of even potential relevance to an ongoing investigation, without reference to its admissibility." (Emphasis in original.) However, the language "may be" would not support a request in which a Contracting State simply asked for information regarding all bank accounts maintained by residents of that Contracting State in the other Contracting State, or even all accounts maintained by its residents with respect to a particular bank.

Exchange of information with respect to each State's domestic law is authorized to the extent that taxation under domestic law is not contrary to the Convention. Thus, for example, information may be exchanged with respect to a covered tax, even if the transaction to which the information relates is a purely domestic transaction in the requesting State and, therefore, the exchange is not made to carry out the Convention. An example of such a case is provided in the OECD Commentary: a company resident in the United States and a company resident in New Zealand transact business between themselves through a third-country resident company. Neither Contracting State has a treaty with the third State. To enforce their internal laws with respect to transactions of their residents with the third-country company (since there is no relevant treaty in force), the Contracting States may exchange information regarding the prices that their residents paid in their transactions with the third-country resident.

Paragraph 1 clarifies that information may be exchanged that relates to the assessment or collection of, the enforcement or prosecution in respect of, or the determination of appeals in relation to, the taxes covered by the Convention. Thus, the competent authorities may request and provide information for cases under examination or criminal investigation, in collection, on appeals, or under prosecution.

The taxes covered by the Convention for purposes of this Article constitute a broader category of taxes than those referred to in Article 2 (Taxes Covered). Exchange of information is authorized with respect to taxes of every kind imposed by a Contracting State at the national level. Accordingly, information may be exchanged with respect to U.S. estate and gift taxes, excise taxes or, with respect to New Zealand, value added taxes.

Information exchange is not restricted by paragraph 1 of Article 1 (General Scope). Accordingly, information may be requested and provided under this article with respect to persons who are not residents of either Contracting State. For example, if a third-country resident has a permanent establishment in New Zealand, and that permanent establishment engages in transactions with a U.S. enterprise, the United States could request information with respect to that permanent establishment, even though the third-country resident is not a resident of either Contracting State. Similarly, if a third-country resident maintains a bank account in New Zealand, and the Internal Revenue Service has reason to believe that funds in that account should have been reported for U.S. tax purposes but have not been so reported, information can be requested from New Zealand with respect to that person's account, even though that person is not the taxpayer under examination.

Although the term "United States" does not encompass U.S. possessions for most purposes of the Convention, section 7651 of the Code authorizes the Internal Revenue Service to utilize the provisions of the Internal Revenue Code to obtain information from the U.S.

possessions pursuant to a proper request made under Article 25. If necessary to obtain requested information, the Internal Revenue Service could issue and enforce an administrative summons to the taxpayer, a tax authority (or a government agency in a U.S. possession), or a third party located in a U.S. possession.

Paragraph 2 of Article 25

Paragraph 2 also provides assurances that any information exchanged will be treated as secret, subject to the same disclosure constraints as information obtained under the laws of the requesting State. Information received may be disclosed only to persons, including courts and administrative bodies, involved in the assessment, collection, or administration of, the enforcement or prosecution in respect of, or the determination of the of appeals in relation to, the taxes covered by the Convention. The information must be used by these persons in connection with the specified functions. Information may also be disclosed to legislative bodies, such as the tax-writing committees of Congress and the Government Accountability Office, engaged in the oversight of the preceding activities. Information received by these bodies must be for use in the performance of their role in overseeing the administration of U.S. tax laws. Information received may be disclosed in public court proceedings or in judicial decisions.

Paragraph 3 of Article 25

Paragraph 3 is in all material respects the same as paragraph 3 of Article 25 of the existing Convention. Paragraph 3 provides that the obligations undertaken in paragraphs 1 and 2 to exchange information do not require a Contracting State to carry out administrative measures that are at variance with the laws or administrative practice of either State. Nor is a Contracting State required to supply information not obtainable under the laws or administrative practice of either State, or to disclose trade secrets or other information, the disclosure of which would be contrary to public policy.

Thus, a requesting State may be denied information from the other State if the information would be obtained pursuant to procedures or measures that are broader than those available in the requesting State. However, the statute of limitations of the Contracting State making the request for information should govern a request for information. Thus, the Contracting State of which the request is made should attempt to obtain the information even if its own statute of limitations has passed. In many cases, relevant information will still exist in the business records of the taxpayer or a third party, even though it is no longer required to be kept for domestic tax purposes.

While paragraph 3 states conditions under which a Contracting State is not obligated to comply with a request from the other Contracting State for information, the requested State is not precluded from providing such information, and may, at its discretion, do so subject to the limitations of its internal law.

Paragraph 4 of Article 25

Paragraph 4 provides that when information is requested by a Contracting State in accordance with this Article, the other Contracting State is obligated to obtain the requested information as if the tax in question were the tax of the requested State, even if that State has no direct tax interest in the case to which the request relates. In the absence of such a paragraph, some taxpayers have argued that paragraph 3(a) prevents a Contracting State from requesting information from a bank or fiduciary that the Contracting State does not need for its own tax purposes. This paragraph clarifies that paragraph 3 does not impose such a restriction and that a Contracting State is not limited to providing only the information that it already has in its own files.

Paragraph 5 of Article 25

Paragraph 5 provides that a Contracting State may not decline to provide information because that information is held by financial institutions, nominees or persons acting in an agency or fiduciary capacity. Thus, paragraph 5 would effectively prevent a Contracting State from relying on paragraph 3 to argue that its domestic bank secrecy laws (or similar legislation relating to disclosure of financial information by financial institutions or intermediaries) override its obligation to provide information under paragraph 1. This paragraph also requires the disclosure of information regarding the beneficial owner of an interest in a person, such as the identity of a beneficial owner of bearer shares.

Paragraph 6 of Article 25

Paragraph 6 provides that the requesting State may specify the form in which information is to be provided (e.g., depositions of witnesses and authenticated copies of original documents). The intention is to ensure that the information may be introduced as evidence in the judicial proceedings of the requesting State. The requested State should, if possible, provide the information in the form requested to the same extent that it can obtain information in that form under its own laws and administrative practices with respect to its own taxes.

Paragraph 7 of Article 25

Paragraph 7 provides for assistance in collection of taxes to the extent necessary to ensure that treaty benefits are enjoyed only by persons entitled to those benefits under the terms of the Convention. Under paragraph 7, a Contracting State will endeavor to collect on behalf of the other State only those amounts necessary to ensure that any exemption or reduced rate of tax at source granted under the Convention by that other State is not enjoyed by persons not entitled to those benefits. For example, if the payer of a U.S.-source portfolio dividend receives a Form W-8BEN or other appropriate documentation from the payee, the withholding agent is permitted to withhold at the portfolio dividend rate of 15 percent. If, however, the addressee is merely acting as a nominee on behalf of a third-country resident, paragraph 7 would obligate the other Contracting State to withhold and remit to the United States the additional tax that should have been collected by the U.S. withholding agent.

This paragraph also makes clear that the Contracting State asked to collect the tax is not obligated, in the process of providing collection assistance, to carry out administrative measures that are different from those used in the collection of its own taxes, or that would be contrary to its sovereignty, security or public policy.

Paragraph 8 of Article 25

Paragraph 8 provides that the requested State shall allow representatives of the applicant State to enter the requested State to interview individuals and examine books and records with the consent of the persons subject to examination.

Treaty effective dates and termination in relation to exchange of information.

Once the Protocol is in force, the competent authority may seek information under the Convention with respect to a year prior to the entry into force of the Protocol. Even if an earlier Convention with more restrictive provisions, or even no Convention, was in effect during the years in which the transaction at issue occurred, the exchange of information provisions of the Protocol apply. In that case, the competent authorities have available to them the full range of information exchange provisions afforded under this Article. Paragraph 3 of Article 28 (Entry into Force) confirms this understanding with respect to the effective date of the Article.

A tax administration may also seek information with respect to a year for which a treaty was in force after the treaty has been terminated. In such a case the ability of the other tax administration to act is limited. The treaty no longer provides authority for the tax administrations to exchange confidential information. They may only exchange information pursuant to domestic law or other international agreement or arrangement.

ARTICLE XV

Article XV of the Protocol deletes and replaces Paragraph 1 of the Protocol to the existing Convention, signed in 1982.

Paragraph 1

With reference to Articles 11 (Interest) and 12 (Royalties) if in any future double taxation convention with any other country New Zealand agrees to limit its taxation at source on any interest or royalties to rates lower than the ones provided in this Convention, then New Zealand shall notify the United States, and the Contracting States shall, at the request of the United States, and without undue delay, consult each other with a view to concluding an additional protocol to incorporate such lower rates into this Convention.

ARTICLE XVI

Article XVI of the Protocol contains the rules for bringing the Protocol into force and giving effect to its provisions.

Paragraph 1

Paragraph 1 provides that the Protocol is subject to ratification in accordance with the applicable procedures of the United States and New Zealand. Further, the Contracting States shall notify each other by written notification, through diplomatic channels, when their respective applicable procedures have been satisfied.

In the United States, the process leading to ratification and entry into force is as follows: Once a treaty has been signed by authorized representatives of the two Contracting States, the Department of State sends the treaty to the President who formally transmits it to the Senate for its advice and consent to ratification, which requires approval by two-thirds of the Senators present and voting. Prior to this vote, however, it generally has been the practice for the Senate Committee on Foreign Relations to hold hearings on the treaty and make a recommendation regarding its approval to the full Senate. Both Government and private sector witnesses may testify at these hearings. After the Senate gives its advice and consent to ratification of the treaty, an instrument of ratification is drafted for the President's signature. The President's signature completes the process in the United States.

Paragraph 2

Paragraph 2 provides that the Protocol will enter into force on the date of the later of the notifications referred to in paragraph 1. The relevant date is the date on the second of these notification documents, and not the date on which the second notification is provided to the other Contracting State. The date on which a treaty enters into force is not necessarily the date on which its provisions take effect. Paragraph 2, therefore, also contains rules that determine when the provisions of the Protocol will have effect.

Under subparagraph 2(a), the Convention will have effect with respect to taxes withheld at source (principally dividends, interest and royalties) for income derived on or after the first day of the second month in the first calendar year following the date on which the Protocol enters into force.

In the United States, for all other taxes, subparagraph 2(b) specifies that the Protocol will have effect for taxes chargeable for any tax year beginning on or after January 1 of the year following entry into force of the Protocol.

In New Zealand, for all other taxes, subparagraph 2(c) specifies that the Protocol will have effect for taxes chargeable for any tax year beginning on or after April 1 of the year following entry into force of the Protocol.

Paragraph 3

The powers afforded under Article 25 (Exchange of Information and Administrative Assistance) apply retroactively to taxable periods preceding entry into force.